GET UP | THE ART OF PERSEVERANCE

ADAM GREENBERG

WITH BEN BIDDICK

www.GetUpNation.com

Cover design by John Bryll Pulido.
Front cover photo credit Steve Mitchell.
Copyright © 2005 Associated Press.
Back cover photo credit Chris Bruno.

Library of Congress Control Number: 2017907335
ISBN: 978-0-9987183-0-9

This book may be purchased in bulk for educational, promotional, or business use. Please contact Mackenzie Daniel by email at getup@mackenziedaniel.com.

First Edition: June 2017

"Adam represents what we all *can* be."

- Matt Lauer, Television Journalist
and host of NBC's *Today*

"If F. Scott Fitzgerald had envisioned Adam Greenberg, he might never have said, 'There are no second acts in American lives.'"

- Willie Weinbaum, ESPN

"Do you know this player Adam Greenberg?" he asked. "Seven years ago, he was a rookie, and in his very first at-bat he got hit in the head with the ball – knocked out, concussed, out of the league." Seinfeld raised an index finger from the wheel: "One pitch." The Marlins had agreed to sign Greenberg for a single day after fans petitioned on his behalf. "It might seem a bit 'Jewy' if I get too excited about it – I wish he wasn't Jewish," Seinfeld said. "But it's a fascinating story. One at-bat after seven years. Think of the pressure on this guy!"

- Jerry Seinfeld, Actor and Comedian

"Adam Greenberg is what you might call a brutal optimist. When he sits across the table and tells his story, the words run so counter to his manner – the words are tragic, the rest of him immutably upbeat. You start imagining that you could travel back in time and airdrop him into history's nastiest infernos just to watch him get up and grin and start plotting his escape."

- Stephen J. Dubner, author "Jewish Jocks" essay
"Once-Hit Wonder", and Co-Author "Freakonomics"

"Adam's story is a reminder to us all about the power of perseverance and overcoming life's biggest challenges. His relentless pursuit of his dream, while allowing himself to lean on the support of others, provides invaluable lessons for life. I am encouraged by Adam's tenacity and resolve, and his courageous journey to return to the plate."

- Robert Wolf, Founder and CEO of 32 Advisors
and Chairman of Measure - Drone as a Service

"Adam Greenberg gets his first at-bat in SEVEN YEARS, and has to face a KNUCKLEBALLER? Who won 20 games?! What kind of a sick joke is that?!"

- Jim Rome Host of CBS
Radio's "Jim Rome Show"

"Former pro-athlete with a supplement company? Hearing this I made all sorts of assumptions, and am happy to report, I was way off the mark. Adam Greenberg's story, and his actions as a person, are inspirational. This book makes me want to get up, keep trying, and in failure, see future success. His message is universal and kind. Read this book."

- Kate Deeks, Editor of "Get Up |
The Art of Perseverance"

I am blessed for all the support I have received from Major League Baseball, the Chicago Cubs, the Miami Marlins, members of the media, my coaches, friends, family, and the loved ones who have persevered through my journey over the years, and for those no longer with us.

This book is dedicated to members of the armed services, law enforcement, and the first responders who persevere through life's most difficult challenges and selflessly put their lives on the line to keep us safe. This book is also for everyone who has ever had a goal, a belief in themselves, and a genuine care for those around them. Most importantly, I dedicate this to my son Leo, and the youth that will make up our future.

Contents

Introduction

On July 9, 2005, I stepped into the batter's box for my first major-league plate appearance with the Chicago Cubs. That moment was the culmination of my life's work and my proudest achievement up to that point. No one suspected the triumph of that moment would be obliterated by a 92 mile-an-hour first-pitch fastball striking me just under my helmet on the back of my head. The first pitch of my major-league career threatened not only the future of my ability to play baseball, but my life itself.

I didn't know it at the time, but that pitch was a gift. What was both the greatest and worst split-second of my life sent me into an odyssey of struggle, pain, and confusion which forged me slowly into the man I am today. What I thought was the destroyer of my dream was actually the birth of a greater one. It took me years to understand it, but it was worth every moment. I would take none of it back.

This book is not simply a baseball story or a story about a baseball player. This book is a beginning. On one level, it is the beginning of my story. As the story of my life intersects with your life, this story will become ours. As we connect, create, persevere, and overcome, our story will become our history. Just like anything in life, to do something well requires practice. The art of getting up is the same.

Maybe this book was handed to you while you lay in a hospital bed grappling with a grim, life-threatening diagnosis or a career-ending injury. Maybe you're teetering on the edge of crushing debt, headed toward imminent bankruptcy, or struggling in the middle of a job search. Maybe you're still grinding it out in a shared workspace, all-in on pursuing your startup dreams but drowning in obstacles and challenges. Maybe you're a student athlete overwhelmed with what seems like never-ending amounts of schoolwork and practice.

No matter what you're doing or what you're facing, I offer you my story of overcoming adversity and persevering through challenges in hopes of helping you relentlessly pursue your dream for your life. Let's strive for a brilliant tomorrow, especially if it's a brutal today. There is nothing we can't do. There is nowhere we can't go. Let's get after it. It's time to Get Up!

– Adam

Part 1 | Love of the Game

"He Gets It from Me!"

Mark and Wendy Greenberg backed out of the driveway and began their drive to Boston from Guilford, Connecticut. Though their son Adam was just 9 years old, they had promised to take him to his first regional karate tournament. Adam was eager to compete, and they agreed to provide him the opportunity. At regionals, he would be facing a larger nexus of more skilled and experienced opponents. For the two-hour drive, Mark and Wendy prepared Adam for how he should handle himself when the inevitable loss came. They tried to ensure his expectations were appropriately tempered. They told him not to expect to win every fight. They reminded him this was a different level of competition than what was available locally in Guilford. Adam also had a friend competing in the tournament. They told him to be gracious if his friend won and to be sure to congratulate him afterward.

Adam had a slightly different plan. By the end of the day, he stood in front of his parents with a first-place trophy standing almost as tall as he did. He'd won it all. His friend was the one congratulating him instead. They began to realize what was inside their child. "He had a burn in him that has never left," Mark said about his son. "He was completely committed."

It wasn't just his athletic ability which surprised his parents. Adam came home one day from elementary school with a problem he wanted to talk about with his parents. Expecting he would tell them he was having trouble with classwork or some fleeting childhood difficulty, they were startled to find out he was having a business dispute with some of his classmates about their profit margin in a candy sale business. Adam had been separating out the bulk candy bags his mother purchased for the family into individual packets and was selling them to his classmates. He hadn't merely started his own business. He'd created an entire distribution network, and some of his classmate distributors wanted a larger share of the profits! As their son looked to them for guidance, Mark and Wendy realized they didn't just have an athlete on their hands, they also had an entrepreneur.

Adam's intense commitment to athletics continued into high school. Mark recalled bringing him home after he played an entire high school baseball game. After dinner, he found him outside taking practice swings with his bat. Surprised that he wasn't relaxing after the game, Adam told him, "I have to work on my bat speed, Dad."

Mark and Wendy continued to invest in their son's interests while using athletics to instill basic values like honesty. They were proud of the man he became because of those lessons and enjoyed watching him pursue his dream of playing Major League Baseball. While he attended the University of North Carolina at Chapel Hill, Wendy put 90,000 miles on her minivan in three years. "We were there to support him, but we did it quietly. He always knew we were there for him. It didn't need to be said. I think that contributed to his confidence. We never forced him to do any of it. We certainly supported him and were intentional about connecting him with opportunities, but it was never something we made him do. It was him. He had a powerful drive to succeed in sports and in life," Mark said.

People began to notice Adam's athletic accomplishments. They admired his speed but were often dismissive when it came to his size. "Adam has always loved to prove people wrong when they limited or dismissed him. He's skilled at making adversity transformative," Mark said. Adam began to realize adversity could be the tool which made him, his teammates, or their circumstances better. "Whenever he got injured, you just knew he was going to come back stronger," Wendy said.

One opportunity Mark and Wendy connected Adam with was the Area Code Games. The Area Code Games are a five-day showcase of the best high school baseball players in the country. This afforded 350 professional scouts and 100 Division I coaches the opportunity to evaluate America's future up and coming players. Wendy described the buzz he created at the Area Code Games and what others identified as the reason for Adam's superior performance. A scout at the games pointed at Adam's chest. "What makes him stand out? It's what he's got in there. His heart." Wendy grinned and offered another conclusion: "It's simple. He gets it from me!"

In Adam's Own Words...

What is it that you *have to have*? I'm not referring to your basic needs like food, shelter, and clothing. I mean, what is the thing you are willing to work so hard for that consumes you to the point you don't even consider taking time off? What are you so hungry for that makes even skipping a workout, practice or study session aversive because it distances you from achieving your dream? If you don't know what this is for you, then now is the time to identify it. I invite you to begin your profound journey today. You don't need to know yet how you will reach what you *have to have*. Just create your vision for it and get going. Once you take action, you'll figure out the details along the way.

My parents never pushed me. They knew the power of *listening*. They guided me through situations by asking what I was thinking and feeling. Parents can turn their kids off to things if they force them to participate in something. By listening closely, they helped identify the passion within me. Once they knew what engaged me, they committed to supporting me in the development toward my goals.

When you truly love something, you invest everything you are and have in order to lay hold of it. As a child, I was captivated by the game of baseball, and I became determined to play this game at the highest level because of how much I loved it. Countless voices dismissed me as too small, too this, too that to reach the major leagues. Those voices fueled the fire burning within me.

– Adam

Exploration and Discovery

In the year 1639, 25 Englishmen burning with a desire for freedom signed a document while on board a ship cutting west across the Atlantic Ocean. It would later be called the Guilford Covenant. Captivated and engaged by the opportunity of freedom, they invested everything they had to realize their dream. They sailed from England toward a place called Quinnipiac, tucked into the western shoreline of what would later become New Haven, Connecticut. With the Guilford Covenant, they pledged to join together to create a settlement called the Plantation of Menunkatuck. This plantation would later be named Guilford, Connecticut, one of the many stones forming the foundation of the United States of America.

Adam Greenberg grew up on *these* shores. The bold heroism of those early explorers infused the ocean, marshes, and woodlands where he played as a child with the belief that anything was possible for men and women who dared to dream big. He developed a respect for those who had the passion and conviction to pursue their dream even in the face of severe opposition and adversity. Adam began to explore this world, wondering what his dream would be, and what his life could become.

"There were two things which engaged me early," Adam said. "Sports and classical music. I don't know why I loved classical music, but sports were my main passion. Whatever season it was, that's what I was playing. If it was soccer season, I spent every waking moment dribbling, juggling, shooting, sprinting, and conditioning. Once basketball season came around, I worked tirelessly before and after practice on every aspect of my game. When winter finally gave way to the spring baseball season, I immersed myself in countless hours of individual tee work, batting practice, speed work, and defensive drills. Most days I didn't even get home until after sunset. I loved being active, and I craved competition. I loved the feeling of all the hard work and preparation paying off with my teammates during my games."

"I grew up watching the Knicks, the Giants, and the Yankees on TV. My hero was Don Mattingly of the Yankees. I idolized him, and I wanted to watch every at-bat. I wanted to know how he fared at the plate every night, what record he broke, everything. I fell asleep at night listening to sports radio. I felt driven to succeed, and I hated to lose. I was competitive with myself. I dreamed of reaching Mattingly's level, of being a professional athlete," Adam said. "As I began to train, I knew I had to work harder than anyone else, and I was willing to do whatever it took to get there. I took baseball bats with me on vacation. While others were enjoying down time, I was sprinting up any hill I could find. If I was going to reach my goal, I knew I had to work hard for it every day. I thought creatively about what I could do to train that I knew no one else was doing. While other people my age spent time and energy doing other things, I was at home doing push-ups and sacrificing comfort to secure the future gain of playing professional baseball."

Adam discovered another love in addition to classical music and sports at a young age. He began exploring his entrepreneurial nature. In addition to his candy sales at school, he put together flyers advertising a business he created called "Adam's Personal Services." He knocked on doors and handed out flyers promising to do odd jobs for his neighbors for a small fee. As he washed cars, moved furniture, and cleaned garages for his neighbors, he found himself interested in their lives and challenges. He enjoyed connecting with his customers while simultaneously delivering a valuable service. He profited financially but also personally as he helped them meet their needs.

When Adam was 13 years old, he began to realize his deepest connection in sports was with the game of baseball. In 1994, he earned a spot on the first Connecticut Amateur Athletic Union (AAU) team. It was comprised of the best players in the state. Earning a spot on the roster was itself a personal eye opener that validated his hard work and commitment to developing as a player. He began to recognize the level of his talent and dream of what was possible.

After nine wins and no losses, Team Connecticut faced Team California for the National Championship at the Field of Dreams in Dyersville, Iowa. Against all odds, Connecticut beat a California team comprised of numerous players who'd populated the 1993 Little League World Series Championship team. Many of them were sons of Major League Baseball players. When Adam realized he could compete against the best and *win*, there was no going back.

Adam remembered watching his teammates celebrating their championship win on the Field of Dreams. As they shouted, hugged, and high-fived, he felt everything change. A Henry Ford quote he'd learned in school entered his mind: "Whether you think you can, or you think you can't, you're right." He began to believe that his dream of playing in the major leagues *was* possible, and he refused to limit himself. As his teammates and opponents walked off the field, Adam inhaled the scent of the green grass and took in every detail. He could see his life before him, fused with fields like this. He removed his cap out of reverence as the setting Midwestern sun bathed the base paths in light. There was no ocean wide, cold, or violent enough to suppress the fire growing within him. He was going to do whatever it took to get there. He was going to join the ranks of his heroes in the major leagues, no matter what it took.

In Adam's Own Words...

Understanding what you *have to have* is the first step of your own unique and meaningful journey. Everyone has one waiting for them. You've been given the incredible gift of life. You have value. If you've ever felt the opposite, then it's my honor to tell you that you are special just the way you are. You're special because you are a distinctly unique human being.

I've always enjoyed when people have counted me out or when someone says something is impossible. These became wonderful opportunities because nothing is impossible. Even during painful times, I continued to invest in the game I loved. The returns were exponential.

– Adam

Mr. Connecticut

At age 13, Adam knew what he wanted to do. The world around him went about its business without knowing there was a young man coming of age in their midst with audacious dreams. The wood was cut, stacked, and drenched in fuel. No one knew he was about to set a fire that would devour every obstacle in his way. He knew he was going to have to *earn* this.

There was no formal baseball training. There were no hired coaches. Other than practices, Adam was completely self-taught in his bedroom, basement, and backyard. "Bat speed. Bat speed. Bat speed," he would chant to himself. He even briefly stepped away from a Bar Mitzvah after-party in Florida while he was a teenager in order to meet his self-inflicted standard of 300 swings per day without fail or holiday.

Adam didn't care if the streets were crusted and slicked with snow and ice. He'd bundle up and attack the hills of Guilford until his lungs burned in the brutal winter air. From tire drag sprints to pull-ups to push-ups, he knew this was the route he had to take. He had to get stronger, faster, more skilled. He worked out tirelessly in the basement while his brothers watched with curiosity and admiration. Adam fought to sharpen and develop every capability he had in a personal crusade against poor and mediocre performance. He would have none of that. He demanded personal excellence.

Adam's brother, Max, described his intense work ethic and drive while he was in high school. "I know it seems like a cliché, but I mean it. I'd never seen anyone work harder." Adam constantly sought out creative ways to improve himself beyond his current physical capabilities. One afternoon as he considered ways he could increase upper body strength, he looked around the room and spotted his youngest brother, Sam. Adam told Sam to climb on his back so he could increase the difficulty of his push-ups beyond his bodyweight. "The amount of time he put in to train himself mentally and physically was second to none," Max said.

One day, Max wandered the family home looking for Adam. It was pouring rain outside, and he realized he hadn't seen his brother in a while. As he passed a window viewing their backyard, movement caught his eye. There was Adam, standing in the family swimming pool, swinging an aluminum bat under the water for more resistance to build bat speed and strength. Torrents of rain ricocheted off the surface of the water, and there he was. Swinging. Resetting. Swinging. Resetting. It didn't matter if it was raining. It didn't matter how loud the thunder growled. What mattered was that every repetition was getting him closer to base hits, doubles, triples, and home runs. It definitely didn't matter to Adam that swinging an aluminum bat outside in a swimming pool during a thunderstorm might not have been the safest of ideas. This level of tireless and extreme dedication is what he knew he needed in order to make it to the major leagues. He could only rest soundly at night when he knew he'd done everything possible that day to achieve his goal.

If he was going to make it, he was going to have to outperform his peers. Not only would he have to beat out the best players from the United States, but he also knew he would have to beat out the best international players. There were only a few *hundred* roster spots available at any one time at the major-league level. Adam was going to earn one, no matter what it took.

Once Adam identified his goal, he began identifying his obstacles. He broke the game down into specific challenges. He turned base stealing into both a science and an art form. The distance between bases is exactly 90 feet, but the margin between out and safe is razor thin. The time allowed to safely steal a base depended heavily on the timing of both the pitcher and catcher. The average time it takes for a catcher to throw from home plate to second base is approximately 2.0 seconds. Major league catchers are even faster. Adam added the amount of time it took from the pitcher's first movement home until the baseball hit the catcher's mitt. If the pitcher took longer than 1.4 seconds to deliver his pitch, he calculated he had a better shot of reaching safely. If the pitcher was quicker, he had to be even faster.

Adam repeated this deconstruction process for every aspect of the game. Not only was he developing himself physically to meet the challenges of the game, he was striving to prepare himself mentally. As his knowledge of the game grew, he began to see how to exploit an opponent's weakness to gain an advantage. He even began to identify his own team's weaknesses and see how strategic decisions could limit damage by the opponent. Adam began to readily identify which moments in the game were most crucial and why. He recognized which pivotal seconds of game time were personal opportunities to help his team win. He could see how his tireless training was paying off in the outfield, batter's box, and on the base paths. Even failures in games and practices served as a guide to additional improvement for Adam and his teammates. He vowed to never stop learning and growing. Every failure and success deepened his all-consuming love of the game.

The hours and intensity of Adam's mental preparation generated phenomenal results. Every time he stepped onto the field he smiled and burned with the thought, "This is where a five foot eight and three quarter inch tall Jewish kid from Guilford, Connecticut, is going to make a name for myself." He fueled himself with voices of the faithless who gave him no shot of achieving his dream. "That Greenberg kid is too small. He'll never play Division I baseball. He's too short. Not enough arm strength. Not enough power. No way."

During Adam's freshman year of high school, he made the varsity soccer, basketball, and baseball teams. He played all three sports every year of his high school career and earned a varsity letter in all 12 seasons. He was chosen to be team captain for baseball and soccer during both his junior and senior years. The accolades continued to roll in. The New Haven Register selected Adam as the 1998-99 Connecticut Male Athlete of the Year. He was the first player in the state of Connecticut to earn All-State baseball honors for four consecutive years.

He was the starting forward for Guilford soccer for four seasons and led the team to a state championship in 1996. In his senior year, he set a school record of 17 assists. He still holds the current Guilford High School career record of 33 total assists. By his senior season he earned All-American, All-New England, All-State, All-Conference and All-New Haven Area honors in multiple seasons. Adam was awarded the Most Valuable Player of the area by the New Haven Register after his senior year. He was also awarded a position on the All-Conference Second Team for his role as the Guilford varsity basketball point guard for the 1998-99 season. He served as the vice president of the athletic leadership committee and played summer baseball with the Madison Legion Post 79 team.

Adam began to see how his individual commitment to excellence led to team accomplishments. "I started to learn about shared work ethic and how leading by example could be a powerful motivator for everyone on the team," he said. "If the team saw one guy really hustling, it would inspire everyone else to reach or surpass that level. We all became better as we collectively worked harder to achieve our individual, absolute best. As a result, we began to accomplish things as a team that we would've never been able to accomplish if it was not for that constant competition and hustle and sweat. That opened up my world. That showed me *how* I could achieve my goal of becoming a professional baseball player. I began to wonder if maybe I found the hidden doorway to the actualization of my dream."

Loren, Adam's younger sister, remembered looking up to her older brother. She remembered pushing herself to excel because of his example and reputation. She remembered how he always found the positive in every situation to propel himself forward. She remembered how people would dismiss him because he was smaller than others he was competing against. He never let it get to him. He was respectful of people who dismissed him, but he let their words fuel his inner fire to prove them wrong. Nothing could stop him. "It was inspiring to me," Loren said. "Adam's resilience reminded me of my grandfather Erwin 'Itch' Harrison who survived being shot down in his airplane during World War II. He endured a lot of struggles, and he never had much of anything, but you'd have thought he had everything."

Max, like Loren, looked up to Adam. When he began his freshman year at Guilford High School, Adam was a senior. He earned a spot on the varsity basketball team as a freshman and was able to play on the same team as his older brother, the team captain. Adam was known throughout the town as an elite athlete. Everyone knew him. Everyone looked up to him, especially Max, who strived to earn the respect of his teammates, uphold the reputation Adam created for their family, and contribute to a team that relentlessly pursued winning.

His sweat and dedication paid off. Max began to earn a greater amount of playing time as the season progressed. During a basketball game against Branford, Guilford's rival, Max and Adam were both on the court as the seconds ticked away. Both teams scrapped for every point as the game neared its end. A Branford player stole a pass which sparked a fast break toward the Guilford rim. Max sprinted the length of the court in defense, a victory hanging in the balance. He was the only Guilford defender standing tall against the onslaught of Branford Hornets swarming toward him.

Max thought of his brother in a torrential downpour swinging a metal bat in a swimming pool to increase bat speed and strength. He thought of Adam telling Sam to sit on his back while he did push-ups because he needed to go beyond mere body weight. He thought of how Adam would quietly set about proving wrong anyone who said he wasn't strong enough, tall enough, big enough, or fast enough. He knew exactly what he should do, the only thing he could do.

Max quickly transitioned from retreat to attack. He raced directly at the Branford player with the ball. He posted both feet and braced for the impact. It didn't matter that Max stood 5-foot 10-inches tall and weighed a mere 115 pounds. It didn't matter that the Branford player storming down the court weighed at least 200 pounds, was cut with muscle, and was closing in on the rim directly behind him. It didn't matter that Max was a freshman, or what his last name was, or the pain that hit him head-on during their collision. He slid across the floor and battled for breath. The referee blasted his whistle calling the Branford player for a charge. Max prevented a game winning score by Branford.

Adam was the first one there snatching his brother's hand, congratulating him. Adam told him to "Get up" and pulled him upward. Adam was so strong that not only did he pull Max to his feet, but his feet left the ground. "I went from flat on my back to up in the air," Max said. The referee returned possession of the ball back to Guilford, and time on the clock ticked to zero. Adrenaline ripped through Max like fire. He had earned more than just a win for his team. He helped earn a win for the team by investing in it and risking his body. Not only had he earned the respect of his honored elder brother, but he'd shared a court with him. They'd won *together*. To have earned the esteem of his brother and to have contributed to a win alongside him was "one of the coolest feelings I've ever had," Max said.

As Adam's high school career drew to a close, the phone started ringing off the hook with college recruiters trying to get his attention. His family began to wonder where they'd be traveling to see him play baseball. Offer letters poured in. Adam studied the offers in front of him from Yale, Harvard, and other top programs and universities across the United States. It was time to make a decision. He began narrowing his search. Which program would give him the best chance of achieving his dream while receiving a top-notch education? During a series of official college visits, he found himself gazing across the campus of the University of North Carolina at Chapel Hill. It felt like home. He felt connected. This was where Adam and his love of baseball would lay the groundwork for his entry into minor league baseball.

In Adam's Own Words...

Once you've identified what you *have to have*, you must take action. It's essential to create a set of measurable, achievable goals that will help you proceed towards your ultimate objective. Whether it's losing 40 pounds, repairing a relationship with a loved one, securing capital for your startup, or making your own run at the major leagues, creating measurable, achievable goals will also help you identify your obstacles.

When you truly love working toward achieving what you *have to have*, the obstacles in your way lose their power. My love for the game of baseball gave me an ability to persevere far beyond even what I thought I was capable of. It was the love of the game that motivated me to continue to practice hours after everyone else hit the showers and went home for the night. It was the love of the game that transformed even my greatest obstacles into some of the greatest gifts in my life.

– Adam

Tar Heel Born

Mike Fox is currently the head baseball coach for the University of North Carolina at Chapel Hill. He has taken the Tar Heels to six College World Series, was Baseball America's National Coach of the Year in 2008, and has been part of all 17 Tar Heel College World Series wins as both a player and coach. Coach Fox continues to lead the UNC baseball program during the most successful era in its history. According to him, Adam is a vital part of that distinguished history. Coach Fox liked Adam immediately. When he arrived for his official visit, Adam looked like he'd just been in a brawl. He thinks fondly of that meeting and will readily tell you that "there's not much not to like about Adam Greenberg."

Coach Fox opened the door to his office and greeted the Greenberg family. Adam looked like he'd been hit by a truck. A few days earlier, an opposing player collided with Adam during a soccer game resulting in a black eye laced with 17 stitches down the side of his face. "Hello, Coach," Adam said. He was recruited by Chad Holbrook who was the assistant coach at the time, so it was the first chance he had to sit down and talk to the head coach of the Tar Heels one-on-one. Adam introduced his parents, and Coach Fox offered them all a seat. After a detailed discussion, they were presented with a scholarship offer. Adam looked at the offer and began to review the details.

Adam didn't want any help from his parents, and he

didn't want any handouts. He'd worked so hard for this opportunity, but the number in front of him was not quite what he was hoping to see. Adam decided to boldly ask Coach Fox, who he'd sat down with for the first time just five minutes ago, if he could have a minute with his parents alone. Adam's heart pounded. Did he really just ask the legendary Coach Fox for a moment of privacy with his parents to discuss the offer? He prepared for the first professional negotiation of his life, measured his emotions, assessed his environment, and prepared to ask for a higher scholarship percentage. When Coach Fox returned, Adam said, "Coach, you'll have 110 percent of me. I just need a little higher percentage on the scholarship." Coach Fox and Adam found a higher number they could agree on. They shook hands. "Let's get this done," Coach said.

Coach Fox appreciated the professional, respectful way Adam carried himself. He wanted him to be a part of what he was building. Adam was entering a higher level of competition and a corresponding higher level of potential reward. To have him agree to a higher number for Adam's presence on the team bolstered his confidence. Now that the offer was signed, Adam prepared to produce results for the team and his coach.

Adam's goals were clear in his mind. He was set on playing centerfield and wanted to hit leadoff. This was an audacious goal for an incoming freshman since the current centerfielder was a returning junior who'd just turned down 1.9 million dollars in the draft to play for the

Yankees. He also played two sports at UNC and was on a full scholarship. Adam knew it was a lofty goal, but he dedicated himself to achieving it. He refused to limit himself and his potential regardless of the circumstance.

Adam was more than just a dedicated player with a lot of talent. Certainly, he was very athletic, high energy, and a strong student from a tight-knit family who played hard. Coach Fox knew he would help the Tar Heels win baseball games. What distinguished Adam was how rapidly he began to separate himself from peers who were also very talented. Players who were already established on the Tar Heel team noticed this too. Adam was confident, possessed high character, and was unbelievably competitive. These traits, fused with a tenacious work ethic, led to intangibles both on and off the field. According to Coach Fox, he was making solid decisions that many 18-year-old men attending a university for the first time don't often make.

Adam practiced and scrimmaged like it was the World Series. He aggressively shagged balls in centerfield. He sprinted, hustled, and sweated through every practice. He knew the culture of the Tar Heel baseball organization said the best person plays regardless of their projected future, graduation year, or level of scholarship. The main question was always, who would help the team win? Adam decided he was going to convince the entire coaching staff and his teammates that he was the best option to win when it came to playing centerfield and hitting leadoff in the spring.

It took some time to adjust. His resolve and confidence would be tested. During off-season scrimmages Adam only got one hit. *One.* He refused to let it get in his head. He worked hard on his approach and timing in extra batting practice. He analyzed his stance and swing during countless hours of tee work. The coaching staff wondered how he would respond and if his confidence would be shaken. "You never know how young men are going to react to adversity," Coach Fox said.

As he navigated his new environment, there were a myriad of challenges off the field as well. College was the first time where Adam encountered religion entering the realm of sports when the team chaplain would recite the Lord's Prayer before games. It was unfamiliar to him because of his Jewish heritage. "None of my teammates were Jewish. I felt different. I felt unique. I felt lucky because my teammates welcomed it and asked questions. It was one of the first times I got to really connect with my Jewish culture and upbringing outside of my home town."

Adam was always respectful of the prayers, and his teammates were respectful of Adam as he shared his Jewish heritage. He explained the significance of the high holidays and other differences between Judaism and other teammates' faiths. After this experience, he began to take a greater interest in understanding what it meant to be Jewish and how it was part of his identity. He found a renewed sense of pride in his culture and the stories of men and women who had endured discrimination, abuse, and even genocide simply because they were Jewish. He developed a strong desire to continue to connect with others while deriving strength from a Jewish culture known for the ability to persevere through a long history of trials and persecution. He quickly became a leader after persevering through a slow start.

In Adam's Own Words...

Team success is what matters, not individual. Whenever we decide to partner up, it's important to evaluate one's individual integrity and ability to work as part of a team. Once two or more people align to create even the smallest of teams, they can achieve exponential results. A carefully designed team, no matter the cause, will help you accomplish anything you put your mind to.

Align over similar core values but expect that good teammates will bring a variety of backgrounds, goals, and interests to the table. Learning to appreciate those differences allows you to succeed with like-minded individuals while drawing from the wisdom of a larger pool of shared experiences. You've found the right mix when there's a natural desire to collectively offer up our skills, talents, or knowledge to the other members of the team.

– Adam

Tar Heel Bred

On their way to Florida in January for the opening games of the season, Coach Fox began to call every player to the front of the team bus in order to issue assignments. Adam noticed the current centerfielder clearly wasn't happy as he made his way back to his seat after meeting with the coach. He glanced out the window of the bus, wondering what it could mean. Had he done enough to earn the leadoff spot in the batting order? Had he been able to convince the coaching staff that his work ethic and performance was sufficient enough to start in center field?

He'd only earned one hit during the fall, but his at-bats were professional. He still found ways to get on base and was constantly in the cages for extra batting practice. He got additional work from the pitching staff when they needed to throw to batters, and he relentlessly worked on his defense and conditioning. He turned every sprint in practice into a race. He wanted to win. He bolted across the field believing that on the other side of those chalk lines was the leadoff spot in the batting order and the opportunity to start in centerfield. If he could scrimmage and practice at this level, then maybe the coaching staff would validate his tenacity.

Coach Fox called Adam's name. He marched to the front of the bus and readied himself for whatever assignment he was given. Coach Fox said he'd decided that Adam would leadoff and play centerfield. His heart began to race. He made his way back to his seat, leaned back, and exhaled. He felt like he could jump out the window and sprint to Florida and beat the team there. Coach told him he'd earned these positions with his ability to read the ball off the bat, his hustle, and his ability to find a way to get on base. It was happening. All the hard work was paying off.

Now that Adam was going to be facing college level pitching, he wondered how it would compare to the level of high school play and competition. He started in centerfield for the first game of the season at the Disney Wide World of Sports complex in Orlando, Florida, as part of the annual Atlantic Coast Conference (ACC) Disney Baseball Blast event. The nine-game event included six ACC teams which were ranked in the nation's top 25. The venue was also where the Atlanta Braves played their spring training games. He soon got his answer.

Adam stepped into the batter's box for his first official plate appearance of the season. It was against a left hander. After a barrage of pitches, he struck out but jogged back to the dugout beaming. He'd seen what the pitcher had, and he knew he could hit it. Adam resolved that just because he struck out, he wasn't going to let anyone beat him in his own head. There were going to be plenty more opportunities. He was going to attack every one of them.

In just his second collegiate at-bat, he hit a triple and tallied two more hits that day to finish 3 for 4 with 3 RBI's. The success of opening weekend continued as he ended up hitting 6 for 12 and made the all-tournament team. Adam's off-season cold streak in the batter's box melted away, and his confidence soared.

Instead of allowing a new team, a higher level of competition, and cultural differences to impede, intimidate, or alienate him, Adam stayed relentlessly positive and applied his tenacious work ethic throughout the ups and downs of his freshman season. He refused to respond to changes with self-pity, bitterness, or excuse. Each challenge became a new opportunity to connect, develop, and achieve. To mire himself in anything other than positivity would dim the reality of his goal to play in the major leagues. "These realities were simply just current challenges. There were challenges before, and certainly there would be more. So be it," Adam said. He consistently reminded himself never to be bogged down with negativity. His tenacious positivity paid off. Even after a midseason slump of 0 for 12, he followed it with a 21-game hitting streak. His performance became electrifying.

By the end of his freshman year, Adam was hitting in the heart of the batting order with a batting average of .386. It was one of the most excellent freshman seasons in all of UNC baseball history. He led all Tar Heels in batting average, hits, runs, triples, stolen bases, and slugging percentage. He hit three leadoff home runs, sustained a 21-game hitting streak, and earned a team high of 34 multi-hit games. Adam's 98 hits tied former major leaguer and UNC alumnus B.J. Surhoff's record for the second-most hits in a single season. He led the ACC in triples. He earned All American honors by the Collegiate Baseball Newspaper and Baseball America. He was selected for both the second team All ACC and the All-Tournament team in the NCAA regionals. Adam also capped off the accolades by being named ACC Rookie of the Year. *If I can play at this level, I'm going to make it to the major leagues,* he began to cautiously allow himself to realize. Adam began to pour fuel on a fire within him that he suspected could burn brighter.

Adam was careful not to let his successes go to his head or breed animosity with teammates. He was committed to the concept that personal achievement was pivotal to team success. Any accolade he received was important in his pursuit of a professional career, but if it didn't translate into team wins, then it was a hollow gain. He stayed committed to success as a team and enjoyed bringing intensity to games and practice because it escalated everyone's potential.

At the end of his freshman season, Adam participated in U.S. National Team trials, then spent the summer with the Wilson Tobs of the Coastal Plain League. It was his first experience in an all wood bat league, and he averaged .255 against some of the best Division I pitchers from across the country. He stole a team high of 15 bases and endured a summer season of what felt like endless bus rides. Adam was hungry to return to campus and start attacking the challenge of his sophomore season.

In Adam's Own Words

I'm proud to be connected to so many great teammates. I've learned that whether on the field or in a board room, we're all connected and our attitudes can directly affect one another in a very positive or negative way. Even the smallest of decisions we make every day in spending our time, energy, and resources can have a direct impact on those around us. I believe success is imminent for those who exude positivity and expect positive outcomes. When that fateful pitch knocked me down, it affected not just me. It affected my teammates, my coaches, my family, the pitcher who threw the ball, the Chicago Cubs organization, baseball fans everywhere, my future wife, and even my future children.

What I chose to do afterwards affected them all as well. When building or joining a new team, it's important to establish connections and partner with those who can help positively guide your actions and support your personal objectives. At UNC, I developed a deep bond not only with my teammates but with the coaching, training, and support staff who brought years of wisdom and perspective that I had yet to experience. They helped train me to better see and deal with the challenges that lay ahead during and after the draft. Partnering with those more experienced than us can help with learning valuable lessons while avoiding, or at least minimizing, mistakes.

- Adam

The Carolina Way

Within hours of reporting back to UNC for his sophomore season, Adam began his intensive weight training regimen. One day as he began a series of decline bench presses with 55 pound dumbbells, another player failed to clear a set of weights out of the way. The dumbbells crashed together with his right hand in between them. Pain seared through his fingers. Adam immediately pulled his hand into his abdomen and cradled his middle and ring finger. He ran into the coach's office with both of his hands clutched together against his chest. The white t-shirt Adam was wearing was covered in blood. "It looked like he'd been shot," Coach Fox recalled. They were soon being sped to the local hospital's emergency room where immediate surgery was recommended.

A hand surgeon fished the severed tendon out of Adam's hand. As he reconstructed his fingers with a variety of screws and stitches, Coach Fox told the surgeon, "You've got to save his hand. This is the ACC Rookie of the Year." Fox remained at Adam's side during surgery to screw the bones in his hand back together while repairing a tendon in his finger.

For the first time, Adam was confronted with a serious injury. The fire inside of him continued to burn, but there was very little he could actively do. Coach Fox wondered how this incident would affect Adam's confidence or ability to play baseball. During the fall, Adam sat the bench and *watched* the game he loved to play. He did incessant finger exercises and researched what he needed to do to overcome the setback of his injury and move forward. The hours and days dragged on as he literally willed the fingers he'd almost lost to heal. He dreamed of being able to grip a bat without pain. Each day Adam wasn't on the field was another day he was unable to continue to develop the skills required to play at the next level.

Adam fought off depression. He focused on what he could control and tried not to become frustrated with what he couldn't. Although he couldn't train to the standard he set for himself, he applied the approach he always did – relentless positivity. How could he grow from this? What was this teaching him? Adam banished negativity, identified what he could do at the present moment, and did it with intensity. *What were the recommendations for rehab? What exercises can I do? How long do I rest, and how long before I can exercise again? I'm down, but I'm getting up. I'm going to get back at it*, he told himself, unwilling to take his eyes off his goal.

When asked how Adam responded to the injury, his mother responded, "Whenever he got hurt, you just knew he was going to come back stronger. He had the ability to develop a tunnel vision where he turned off all negatives and focused entirely on reaching his goal." She never doubted that this was just a minor obstacle that her son would sprint right through because he never doubted himself and his abilities.

Adam didn't disappoint. Despite losing time to recover

after reconstructive hand surgery, he again was among the team leaders in runs, hits, doubles, triples, walks, and stolen bases. Adam's batting average was .310 by the end of his sophomore year. He led the team with a .444 on-base percentage. He tallied 24 runs scored, eight doubles, and three triples in 24 ACC conference games. Adam stole more bases than any other player in the Atlantic Coast Conference that year. He closed out the season by hitting safely in 10 of the final 11 games of the year.

Like a long line of eventual major leaguers, Adam had earned the right to play in the Cape Cod League for the summer with the Chatham A's. Against the very top Division I players in the country, he batted .269 with 32 hits and 7 stolen bases in 38 games. Adam was playing the game he loved at the highest level and on the biggest stage, while seizing every opportunity he could to earn the attention of pro scouts heading into his all-important junior year. He was eligible for the MLB draft after his junior season. He knew he had to be on someone's radar.

One person who noticed Adam's performance was Peter Gammons. Gammons is a Hall of Fame columnist who has covered the game of baseball for Sports Illustrated, the Sporting News, the Boston Globe, ESPN, and the MLB Network. He is an alumnus of the University of North Carolina at Chapel Hill. He was voted National Sportswriter of the Year in 1989, 1990, and 1993 by the National Sportscasters and Sportswriters Association. He was awarded an honorary Poynter Fellow from Yale

University. He also received the 2004 J.G. Taylor Spink Award for outstanding writing from the Baseball Writers Association of America.

Gammons recalled meeting Adam along with his friend and teammate Matt Murton while they played in the Cape Cod League. Everyone was telling Gammons about how great Adam and Matt were. Everyone wanted to play with Adam, and he knew why after meeting him. "He had a great personality. He was respectful," Gammons recalled. "Adam must've been the most popular kid in the league when he played on the Cape."

Adam returned to Chapel Hill for his junior season. He enjoyed a full fall season of strength training after recovering from the injury as a sophomore. Adam was able to reach the physical standards he set for himself that year. Now with his injury well behind him, he put up impressive numbers the following spring. He led the ACC in triples and made the All-Conference Team. He scored 80 runs, earned 90 hits, batted in 57 runs, hit 17 home runs, and averaged .337 with an on-base percentage of .440. He stole 35 bases. The Jewish Sports Review awarded him First Team All-American. As the sun set on his junior year in May 2002, Adam turned his full attention to the Major League Baseball draft.

He wondered if this could be his year. He wondered what interest his performance created in professional teams. He wondered whether he would take the opportunity if offered or if he would stay and complete his college degree. Embedded in these spectacular questions were the next steps leading Adam toward his dream. His phone began to ring.

In Adam's Own Words...

Whenever adversity strikes, there is always potential for improvement and something positive to come out of the situation. I have been fortunate to be surrounded by friends, family, colleagues, teammates, specialists, and coaching staff who have genuinely helped me through adversity without expecting anything in return. I'm always looking to do the same because I've learned that when we put our own interests aside and truly care for others, magical things start to happen.

Choosing to be giving and helpful to others facing adversity is an intentional sacrifice of our own comfort and convenience for someone else's benefit. I have many fond memories of those in my life who have been a steadying presence or a trusted advisor. They've been quick to lend a kind word or encouragement when I needed it and asked for nothing in return. We need encouragement and kindness in our lives like we need oxygen. It's the encouragement and positivity from others that can motivate us to get back up and keep going, no matter the odds.

– Adam

The Ninth Round

Adam's sister Keri remembered watching her younger brother as the house phone finally rang. The living room fell eerily quiet. He'd accomplished so much during high school and continued to perform at such a high level throughout his time in college. Was her kid brother finally about to realize his dream of being drafted? She wondered what team's jersey he'd soon be wearing.

Adam nodded his head and listened intently. "Welcome to the Cubs organization, Adam." He could barely hold onto the phone. This was the call he'd visualized in his mind thousands of times, and it was finally here. He'd been drafted in the ninth round by the Chicago Cubs. They invited him to play on their minor league team in Lansing, Michigan. If he worked as hard as he did in college, he may earn a chance to play at Wrigley Field in the major leagues. The slumps, the setbacks, and the surgery made this moment that much more satisfying. It wasn't easy, but his dream was coming true. It was the opportunity of Adam's lifetime. He set the phone down and held his head in his hands as his immediate family rushed to congratulate him.

Keri smiled. Adam persevered during his time in college without shedding his relentless positivity. His dream was getting closer. Her brother, with all his energy and belief, achieved what he'd been striving for since his first sprints through their neighborhood in Guilford.

41

Every person who told him he wasn't big enough or talented enough for Division I baseball were silenced. Now he would have a whole new level of skeptics to convince in the minor leagues.

Adam decided to forego his last year of college. It was a difficult decision. He was walking away from a degree, a possible College World Series, and a chance to break a battery of records at the university. This was his dream, and he was officially all in. He was issued a bonus check of $78,000 and reported to Lansing, Michigan, to play for the Cub's Class-A minor league team, the Lansing Lugnuts.

After being drafted, Coach Fox remembered hearing Adam tell him, "I'm going to make it to the big leagues, Coach." He wasn't cocky or arrogant. He was just determined. His eyes were on his goal, and nothing was going to stop him. Adam never fully unpacked. He'd skim a shirt off the top of his bag, grab it and go like he was stealing second base. No matter where he laid his head for the night, he refused to allow himself to get comfortable enough to empty his entire bag. The day Adam emptied it would be the day he signed a Major League Baseball contract. That was his destination.

Or was it? He got little playing time in Lansing, and he wrestled to find his role on the team. Within the first few weeks of his arrival, there was a period when Adam sat the bench for eight straight games. No at-bats. No opportunities for stolen bases or diving catches. Nothing. It was a difficult time. Did the coaches not think he was good enough? How was he going to advance if he didn't even get time to play? He'd walked away from what promised to be an epic senior year at UNC for *this*?

"The fire within me was burning me up. I needed to redirect it. During the eighth straight game without seeing the field, I found a mirror in the clubhouse bathroom and squared myself up," Adam said. He looked at himself in a mirror. *Baseball didn't pick me. I picked baseball. I walked away from a college degree, a chance to break records, and a potential College World Series run for a reason. Get out of your own head, Greenberg. Get up. Stay ready. You will get an opportunity,* he told himself. Self-doubt, fear, anxiety, and a teetering confidence fled as Adam called them out one by one and banished them from his mind. Later that night, his phone lit up. Coach wanted him in the office first thing the next morning. Adam endured the night and sat himself down in front of his new coach who barely knew who he was. "Adam," the coach said, "You're getting promoted to Daytona."

In Adam's Own Words...

If you are having trouble identifying what you *have to have*, spend time thinking about what you truly love. Ask yourself, what is it you are passionate about? What do your friends and family notice you always doing? What do you find yourself eager to always talk or learn about? What is something that upsets or disturbs you if you don't have it? What event or activity did you skip recently that leaves you with a nagging irritation like you missed something valuable? These are the questions that create the lens for your own personal vision. This lens will help you focus on what you truly *have to have*.

Once you find your passion, go after it with everything you have, the journey will not always be smooth. The obstacles, failures, successes, and lessons learned will also open the door to people and relationships that would have never been a part of your life without going for it. I never would've learned the greatest lessons of my life or met some of the finest people I have ever known without perseverance and focus.

– Adam

"Suspect" to Prospect

The Lugnuts were having a successful year and playing time was scarce. They went on to finish the 2002 regular season in third place and eventually lost in the final round of the playoffs. The High-A Daytona Cubs were having a down year and were on their way to finishing well below the .500 mark. They were in second-to-last place in the East Division of the Florida State League. "Instead of feeling sorry and telling myself I was trash and couldn't play on one of the best teams in the minor leagues, I told myself that this was my opportunity," Adam said. *If I would get more playing time there, then this was my chance. Forget everything else. Just produce wherever you are and wherever you land. Make the most of each moment. Prove anyone wrong that doubts you can play this game at the highest level,* he thought to himself.

After squaring off in the mirror and refusing to give in even momentarily to hopelessness in Lansing, Adam made his way to Daytona for the remainder of the 2002 season. His new manager was Dave Trembley who would eventually go on to manage the Baltimore Orioles. Trembley's managerial approach was "Show up on time, play hard, bunt and steal when you want," Adam said. This invigorated him because it fit his all-out style of play perfectly. "It was like the reins were taken off," he said. "I could be the ball player I knew I could be."

Adam continued to demonstrate his belief that true champions approach every play with everything they've got regardless of who's watching. He took the field every day by channeling the pent-up fire which only weeks ago threatened to engulf him in Lansing. He viewed every play as a moment to showcase his skills and prove he deserved a shot to play in the Majors.

Adam didn't know it at the time, but in a Saturday evening contest against the visiting St. Lucie Mets, a High-A affiliate of the New York Mets, he would ink his name forever in the record books of professional baseball. He also didn't know at the time that in attendance would be some of the most influential scouts, cross checkers, and top advisors from within the Cubs organization. His years of hard work and preparation were about to collide head on with opportunity.

On August 17, 2002, in Adam's seventh game with the Daytona Cubs, he stepped into the batter's box to lead off the bottom of the first inning and promptly powered a homerun over the right field wall to start the game. "Runs tend to come in bunches and leadoff hits have a way of inspiring an entire lineup," Adam said. He loved being that inspirational spark for his team.

Adam quickly found himself back in the batter's box in the bottom of the second inning. He smacked a two-run triple for his second at-bat, but his offensive onslaught had only begun. In the fourth inning, he noticed the third baseman was playing deeper than usual. Adam stepped in and dropped a picture-perfect bunt down the third base line. He reached first base safely for an infield bunt single.

Buzz of Adam potentially hitting for a cycle began to spread among those in attendance. He already had his single, his triple, and his home run, and it was only the fourth inning! All he needed was a double. Daytona ended up batting around and within the same inning, Adam again stepped into the batter's box for his fourth at-bat of the game. The Mets switched pitchers, bringing in a lefty in an effort to cool off Adam and the red-hot Cubs.

It didn't matter who they put on that mound. Adam couldn't be stopped. He scanned the positioning of the infield defense and confidently tapped home plate with his bat, daring the pitcher to deal his finest pitch. It was belt high as it raced toward the plate. The ball rocketed off Adam's bat, impossible to defend as it ricocheted off the outfield wall. Dave Trembley held up the runner at third in front of Adam and grinned ear-to-ear as he reached second base. He dug his cleats in safely for a stand-up double as the crowd erupted. His teammates celebrated, high-fiving each other, and shouting "Greeny!" Adam had hit for the cycle in just four innings, tying the record for the fastest cycle in professional baseball history, and the first in a Daytona uniform.

The Cubs scouts smiled at each other, glanced down, and quickly put their pencils to work. They were seeing Adam for who he truly was, both offensively and defensively. By the time it was all over, Daytona landed a 17-1 victory over St. Lucie, with Adam contributing a 5 for 6 day at the plate, four RBIs, five runs scored, and three diving catches in the outfield. He was fueled and firing on all cylinders. His stock had just officially climbed from "suspect" to prospect. He continued his blazing performance for the remainder of the 2002 season, securing a .384 overall batting average, a .500 on-base percentage, and 15 stolen bases in 21 games.

Riding this wave of momentum into the off-season, Adam wasted no time in his preparation for the following spring. He conducted daily workouts both on and off the field. He was optimistic and would do whatever it took to continue to advance. He didn't know that this wave was about to crash. During an ordinary weightlifting session, he felt a pop in his left wrist. Pain seared the nerves in Adam's wrist and forearm. The thought of potential surgery loomed. He wondered how long his dream would be delayed. He wasn't able to lift a pitcher of water, let alone wield a baseball bat.

Adam again found himself in a medical exam room getting an MRI. He ran his finger over the surgical scar on his hand while he waited for the results. His mind wandered back to the weight lifting injury in college. "I will push through this," he thought to himself. "I won't let this get me down." The results were in, and the MRI revealed a Triangular Fibrocartilage Complex (TFCC) tear. TFCC is a cartilage structure located on the side of the wrist that keeps the forearm bones stable when the hand grasps or the forearm rotates. He needed surgery. It was time again to persevere through rehab, make the most of this opportunity by getting healthy, and prepare for the 2003 season.

As Adam worked to get back through rigorous rehab, he sought out other channels to occupy his mind to prevent stagnancy during the off-season. He began to tap into his entrepreneurial interests. Delving into his savings, he found a mentor for purchasing pre-foreclosure real estate properties he could fix up to either rent or sell at a profit. It became a profitable side project which supplemented his minor league salary. It also helped him balance the frustration of waiting for his body to heal yet again in order to get back to playing the game he loved. Instead of languishing through rehab and cross country bus rides at the start of the next season, he transformed the discomfort into opportunity and used the time to find and develop more real estate. He made it back in 2003 in time to play healthy for 72 games while hitting for a solid .299 average. He stole 26 bases in 35 attempts. His on-base percentage was .387.

As the 2004 season began, Adam pulled on his Daytona uniform and prepared to execute at the highest level of his career. It was opening day, and he'd never been so close. This could be the year he made it to the major leagues. He hustled on every play, just as he'd done every day of his life.

Adam was on third base. The coach signaled a contact play in an attempt to put pressure on the defense and force in a quick run. Similar to a safety-squeeze play, Adam knew his job was to break for home as soon as his teammate was able to put a good ground ball in play. His teammate succeeded and made contact. Adam instinctively bolted down the third base line to take advantage of his small window of opportunity to score. In his effort to beat the throw, he slid safely over home plate with his left leg. His leg exploded with pain. The play happened so fast that his teammate's bat was still on the ground and hadn't been cleared away from the area as he slid through the dirt. Adam hadn't seen the bat and his leg rolled over the top of it at full speed and with his full bodyweight. He limped off the field in agony and again found himself face to face with the team doctor. He was diagnosed with a severe hematoma. A portion of his leg turned black after a drain was placed as part of the initial treatment. He traveled back to Chicago for more surgery to remove dead tissue.

Adam flew home to recover after a successful surgery but soon developed a life-threatening infection. His doctors worked quickly to prescribe a heavy dose of antibiotics. Adam waited anxiously for his leg to heal while the days dragged themselves along. He felt like his career was passing him by. He counted the days, hours, and minutes before he could get back on the field and start earning his way to the major leagues again. Self-pity tried to slither its way into Adam's mind as others around him began to get called up to begin their careers at the next level.

Frustration began to surface. As with his previous recovery periods, Adam refused to let days go by without being productive. He continued to focus on his property development business to pass the time and supplement his meager income. Every dollar counted as his salary was a mere $1,050 per month plus road trip meal money.

Adam returned to Daytona once he was medically cleared to play. He picked right back up where he left off, averaging .291 in 91 games for Daytona with an on-base percentage of .381. He tied for the most triples in the Florida State League with 12. A promotion followed, and he was moved up to Double-A with the West Tennessee Diamond Jaxx. He continued to produce at the plate averaging .277 in 32 games. By the time the season was over, Adam earned 14 triples which tied him for the third most triples in all of minor league baseball. Momentum was on his side again, this time climbing all the way up to a spot for a game with the Triple-A Iowa Cubs to end the season. He dreamed of a major league call-up.

His in-season success created an opportunity for Adam to play in Arizona with the Mesa Solar Sox, a team comprised of rising stars from the Chicago Cubs, Chicago White Sox, St. Louis Cardinals, Colorado Rockies, and Tampa Bay Rays. Major league organizations sent their top prospects to the Arizona Fall League each year to continue to play and develop during the off-season. Adam excelled with the Solar Sox and opened the eyes of Dusty Baker and others in the Cubs organization. This led to an invitation to participate in major league spring training with the Cubs to start the following season.

After averaging .500 during spring training, his career was finally taking off. Adam continued to find success in

2005 for the Diamond Jaxx, averaging .269 in 95 games with an on-base percentage of .386, 9 triples, and 15 stolen bases. Since enduring an early string of injuries, Adam was finally pain free and healthy. He knew all he needed to do was continue to hustle and produce at the plate. He could taste it. His dream was right there in front of him.

In Adam's Own Words…

Do you like to be micro-managed? Probably not. I've found that micro-management tends to be fear and anxiety based. No one can grow when we are treated as an incompetent liability. When I played for Dave Trembley, I thrived because the environment he created allowed me to be the best version of myself. I achieved so much because I wasn't unnecessarily impeded with petty, irrelevant fear-based obstacles. I was allowed to think, act, learn, and grow.

Pain can be an incredibly effective teacher. If we listen, it can tell us when something is wrong. When we're injured our body immediately swells in an attempt to immobilize the injury because continued movement may only complicate and worsen the situation. When we realize something's wrong in our lives, our discomfort can cause us to search for the source in order to resolve it. In those moments of pain, it's important to objectively look at the situation and not just lash out or run away. Why run? It's an opportunity to identify and understand what creates our pain, then learn and grow from it. If you have a problem, bring a solution, otherwise you're just complaining.

Once we identify the source, we can create a strategy to remove the pain. Being proactive can also help us prevent similar situations in the future. You probably know people who would rather cope with pain by complaining, but I believe people flourish in fearless and constructive environments where complaining doesn't exist. By being proactive, fearless, and constructive, we move past the pain and put ourselves in positions to advance or succeed after learning important lessons. Champions do this well.

– Adam

Welcome to the Show

Adam glanced over the lineup card in preparation for a 13-hour bus ride to Jacksonville, Florida, for an away game road trip. His name was missing from the leadoff spot. In fact, it was nowhere to be found. On further review, he didn't see his teammate Matt Murton's name either. Adam looked at Matt, the card, and back to Matt. "Why aren't we playing?"

They approached Coach Dickerson and asked him why they weren't on the lineup card. Dickerson muttered an excuse and told them, "You're not going to Jacksonville." Adam looked at Matt for a moment and walked away. "Were they getting promoted to Triple-A? Were they getting traded?" Something was up. Always trying to find the positive, Adam told Matt that at least it looked like they were going to avoid a long bus ride. They headed back to their room. The phone rang. It was Keith Miller.

Keith is a sports agent at Seth and Sam Levinson's ACES agency who represent some of baseball's biggest names. Miller is also a former professional baseball player. He played a total of nine seasons in the major leagues for the New York Mets and the Kansas City Royals. He was Adam's agent as he ascended through the minor leagues onto the Chicago Cub roster in July of 2005. "I first met Adam when he was playing in the Cape Cod League. Adam stood out because he wasn't huge. He wasn't 6 foot 5 inches tall, 250 pounds, and bombing 500-foot home runs. He had defense, speed, and hustle. He had an all-out style of play," Miller said. "Adam brought everything a club wants."

A cryptic conversation with Keith concluded with "Root against the Cubs like you never have before." Suddenly brand new hard-core *anti*-Cubs fans, they quickly turned on the TV and found the game. The Cubs lost six games in a row prior to that night's doubleheader, and they'd already lost the first one that night. Jeff Francoeur, of the Atlanta Braves, stepped into the batter's box in the bottom of the eighth inning. He belted a go-ahead home run in the second game of the doubleheader, handing the Cubs their eighth straight loss. Matt and Adam started high-fiving and cheering, though they still had no idea why.

They didn't have to wait long. Literally as soon as the game ended, Adam's phone lit up. It was Coach Dickerson. He told Adam to put the phone on speaker so Matt could hear also. "Adam, Matt, pack your stuff. You're going to be on a plane tomorrow to Florida." For half a second, disappointment began to set in as they assumed they were going to join back up with the Diamond Jaxx who were on their way to Jacksonville by bus. Dickerson added, "You're going to Miami to play with the Chicago Cubs. Congratulations, you've made it to the major leagues."

"The world stopped," Adam said. "It was the most magical moment of my life." Adam and Matt leapt to their feet, hugged, and jumped around the room. The day had finally come. He imagined that call a hundred thousand times in his mind, and suddenly it was real. "At the time, the Cubs were looking for a spark. Teams don't bring up guys that young unless they can provide a spark. That's what they expected him to be," Keith said.

Adam worked to be the "best defensive player on the field and the best base runner" by bringing "not only his energy onto the field, but his intelligence," Keith continued. "Adam was such a great defender and base runner not just by being fast. It was his knowledge of the game." He overcame his smaller physical stature by finding a way. "I knew Adam was going to be successful, whether it was in baseball or in anything else he decided to do, because of his passion."

As they began to pack, Adam thought about all the players he'd met and played with before who received that same call. Everyone was always happy for the guy that got called up, but privately everyone wished it was them. Now it *was* him. To have gotten the call at the same time as Matt made it that much more meaningful. Sharing the same emotions simultaneously was a phenomenal feeling. Of the small fraternity of players who ever had the chance to play Major League Baseball, he wondered how many were called up at the exact same time as one of their teammates and good friends.

"I called and congratulated them. It was so great to see two friends getting called up together like that," Peter

Gammons recalled, expecting Adam to have a decade in the major leagues. "He was a good hitter. He could run, play defense. I thought he'd be there for at least eight to ten years."

Joyful phone calls blazed through New England as Adam notified his friends and family. Appointments were cancelled, and plane tickets were purchased as they hurriedly packed and figured out where they needed to be and when. Max was driving up from Washington, D.C. to link up with the family. They would all leave together from Connecticut. Keri had a licensure exam she couldn't miss. Her heart sank. She was not going to be able to be there, but Loren would keep her in the loop via cellphone. Max congratulated his brother and looked forward to seeing him in Miami. Adam's proud parents shook their heads, smiling. Sam loaded up their luggage in the car. Adam had done what he set out to do. He was a Major League Baseball player!

Adam and Matt sat in their room. It took them all of ten minutes to pack. Now what were they supposed to do? Adrenaline rushed through each of their bloodstreams. They tuned into ESPN just in time to hear Peter Gammons spreading the news on Baseball Tonight. Baseball fans all over the world were being put on notice that Adam Greenberg and Matt Murton were major leaguers. It was surreal.

Matt prepared to get some rest while Adam's mind continued to race. He stared at the ceiling of the hotel room and revisited every step of his journey to this point.

He savored every high and low. He thought of the pain of each injury and each setback. He thought about the thrill he felt each time he stepped back onto the field afterward, ready for all the challenges the game would throw at him, invigorated to respond and compete. His love of the game never left him. Adam thought back to his decision to pursue baseball at age 13, to the Field of Dreams tournament in Iowa, to Coach Fox shaking his hand, to the 12-hour bus rides between towns where he got to play the glorious game he loved for three sensational hours. He closed his eyes and thought about the game he'd dedicated his life to mastering.

Adam marveled at its beauty. He thought about how difficult and satisfying it was to put a pitched ball less than three inches wide into play within three tenths of a second. It was nearly mystical pleasure to make solid contact with a pitch, when it felt like the ball melted into the bat before his victorious sprint toward first base. To step into a batter's box in the major leagues would mean facing the masters of the game. With one swing of the bat, anything became possible. There was very little Adam wanted more.

This was the moment that made all the hard work worth it. He had longed to play the game at this level. It engaged his mind completely. He loved to see the strategy form and develop as the game evolved. He worked hard to find advantages and exploit them with speed and confidence, knowing one play could change an entire game. Adam craved hearing the crack of the bat from the outfield. Each time was a new opportunity to challenge the laws of physics with supreme athleticism.

Utilizing his speed was one of Adam's favorite endeavors. He savored the art of stealing a base and the attention to detail it took to be successful. He loved getting a good read on the pitcher and good jump, every muscle primed to take off, in flight, his cleats barely touching the dirt as he flew, covering 90 feet in mere seconds. This was a game of inches and tenths of seconds, and Adam loved every bit of it.

Lying in bed thinking of all that was behind him, and what was to come, his heart pounded. His mind was on fire. He was going to the major leagues! Adam looked over at Matt who had fallen asleep. *How is that possible,* he thought. *How can he sleep?*

The next morning, they hailed a taxi and checked in at the airport. Adam glanced at his flight pass and noticed "First Class" at the top of the ticket. He took his seat in the front of the plane for the first time in his life and smiled. He wasn't crammed into a bus seat wondering how he would pass the next 12 hours. He'd be in Florida in just a few hours to join his new team, the Chicago Cubs.

In Adam's Own Words...

Facing adversity is guaranteed in this life. We must not give it more power than it deserves. Trauma can terrify us, but we must not let it paralyze us. We must grow from it and find the gift inside of it. One practical way to do this is by celebrating the good times. I liken this to my experience of getting called up at the same time as Matt. It was one of the most profound joys of my life and I'm grateful to have had that epic experience in the company of a close teammate who was experiencing the exact same thing.

– Adam

Go Cubs Go!

Adam walked into the clubhouse and was greeted with a Cubs uniform with the number 17 on it. The famous first baseman Mark Grace wore that number, and now it was Adam's. His contract lay before him, which he promptly signed. He would be earning the pro-rated major league minimum salary of $316,000. That was fine with Adam. It was more than 10 times what he was making a week ago. The Cubs traveling secretary handed him an envelope full of cash. He said, "Here's some meal money for a few days." Adam glanced inside. It was more money than he'd earned in an entire month playing minor league ball. He looked up at him and paused.

"What? You don't want it?" the secretary asked. Adam shoved the envelope in his pocket and kept moving down the line to get assigned equipment, sign forms, and get familiarized with where he needed to go and when. He felt relief pour through him. Baseball was never about the money, but all the stress associated with living paycheck to paycheck at poverty-level was gone. He was free to focus on the game he loved. He was free to immerse himself into performing at a major league level.

Dusty Baker is currently the manager of the Washington Nationals. He previously managed the San Francisco Giants, and the Cincinnati Reds, as well as the Chicago Cubs when Adam was called up. He was the National League Manager of the Year in 1993, 1997 and

2000. Prior to coaching, he spent 19 years playing professionally with the Atlanta Braves, Los Angeles Dodgers, San Francisco Giants and Oakland Athletics. He was voted the National League Championship Series MVP in 1977. He won a World Series ring and a Gold Glove with the Los Angeles Dodgers in 1981. He earned Silver Slugger Awards in 1980 and 1981 and was an All-Star in 1981 and 1982. Dusty also served proudly in the United States Marine Corps Reserve from 1969 through 1975.

As Adam ascended the ranks of the minor leagues, Baker recalled him being a tough out. He remembered watching him routinely see 10 or more pitches during an at-bat. "That showed me what kind of person he was," he said. "He was a fighter, but intelligent. A lot of fighters are just physical guys. Adam was a mental and physical fighter. He came to work every day and hustled. He's also a spiritual man who knows how to combine all those attributes together."

Dusty called Adam and Matt into his office. He informed them Matt would play that night, and Adam would have the night off. Adam wasn't complaining. He barely slept at all during the last 24 hours. For the first time in his life, Adam welcomed the extra downtime to recover and prepare. He strolled through the brilliant Florida sun into the Marriott where the team was staying to get settled before the game. He could smell the Biscayne Bay breeze blowing through the lobby. He opened the door to his suite. A congratulatory note from Keith Miller was propped next to a bottle of Dom Perignon on ice.

Adam set down his bag on the hotel bed. In sacred silence, he unpacked *every* item. He slid shut the closet, bathroom, and bureau drawers and looked at the empty shell of the bag. Adam never saw it so flat and wilted. He smiled. It was officially empty and fully unpacked. He was a Chicago Cub. He'd kept his promise to himself. He'd made it, and this was where he was determined to stay.

The sky darkened. Hurricane Dennis loomed in the Gulf of Mexico, delivering a battery of rainclouds across the Florida horizon. Rain drenched the field as Adam arrived early to prepare for the game. On-field batting practice was cancelled, so he warmed up inside the team tunnel. His opportunity to step into a major league batter's box, even if just to practice, would have to wait for another day.

Adam focused on enjoying every second with his new team. The players in the clubhouse were happy to see him. He felt validated and empowered as they welcomed him. Although he wasn't in the lineup the first night, he stayed ready for his turn. He looked forward to getting his shot to contribute to the team.

Baker remembered when he was new to the majors and how badly he wanted to get into the games. "It didn't matter who I was facing," he said. He recalled one night facing Nolan Ryan who was "wild and throwing 100 miles an hour." Baker remembered his coach glancing through the dugout looking for someone to pinch hit. "Suddenly guys were tying their shoes, going to the bathroom, or going to get some water. But I was like, 'Choose me!' That's how I recall Adam was. He's different than most young men."

Baker believed it was important for rookies to have at-bats in front of their parents. "Some other managers don't care about that, but I do," he said. He remembered immediately going to a pay phone after one of his first major league games to call his father. He fondly recalled what it meant to tell him about the double he hit during the game.

The next night, July 9, 2005, Adam stretched throughout the game, staying loose. He knew his time could come at any moment. He couldn't wait to fuse a lifetime of preparation with such an epic opportunity. His batting gloves stayed on, and his bat was at his side through every inning. As a left-handed hitter, Adam knew his best chance of getting into the game as a pinch hitter would be against a right-handed pitcher. As the top of the ninth inning arrived, his heart sank when the Marlins put a left-handed reliever on the mound named Valerio De Los Santos. Baker needed a pinch hitter. He was aware that Adam's parents were in the stands and knew immediately who to select. "Adam didn't care how tough the pitcher was. He wanted an at-bat."

To Adam's surprise, Dick Pole, the Cubs bench coach, barked his name. "Greeny, get a bat. You're hitting for the pitcher." Adam snapped into action without hesitation. This was it! He wasn't nervous or overly excited. This was as normal as walking or breathing. He prepared for this at-bat thousands of times. He slid the batting helmet onto his head and immediately noticed something was different from the minor league helmets he was used to wearing. The major league helmet only had one ear flap. It fit so well he barely knew it was on. Dusty shifted the toothpick in his mouth, told Adam to get on base, then added, "Go get 'em, kid."

The Cubs were on top by two runs. De Los Santos stood on the pitcher's mound, his jersey rippling in the breeze. Adam studied him from the on-deck circle. He knew from the scouting report Valerio threw hard and often used a sharp breaking ball. Tonight was going to be his first major league hit, he told himself. It was his job to get on base. Todd Hollandsworth grounded out and headed back to the dugout. Adam was up. He strode toward the batter's box and announced himself to the umpire. "For the pitcher," he said, digging in.

In Adam's Own Words...

There must be rewards along the way which make all the hard work worth it. Sometimes the work itself is the celebration. I don't know how many times I looked around the stadium during practice, after hours, or at dawn and considered how sensational it was just to be there. Teammates often would ask me why I was smiling so big when our lungs were burning for oxygen after sprints and sweat was pouring off of us during drills. The answer was simple. I was playing the game I loved, and I loved every second of it, especially the preparation.

What is it that you are thankful for right now? Your children? Your spouse? Your health? Your income? Celebrate it and be grateful. Just never allow yourself to become so satisfied that you suppress your drive to be healthier, a better parent, a better spouse, or more effective at your job. Better health means longer life, less pain, and decreased limitations. Better parenting leads to richer legacies and the ultimate gift of guiding a life that's been given to you. Investments in your most intimate relationships build trust, joy, satisfaction, and peace. More income means an increased ability to help empower others, to give back, and to create. Celebrate to create a continued state of gratitude. Celebrate to keep from taking things for granted. Celebrate because you never know when another opportunity to persevere is looming right around the corner.

 – Adam

Man Down

The Florida air was humid. The field gleamed underneath the lights. This ballpark was different from others he'd played on. The Miami Dolphins football team also played here so the field dimensions felt slightly off. The center field distance marker wasn't in its usual position. Adam eyed the center fielder, Juan Pierre, who was shading him toward left.

Adam recalled his first experience pinch hitting. It was during spring training in 2003 against the three-time All-Star pitcher Tom Gordon. Gordon threw Adam a 95 mile-per-hour fastball right down the middle. Adam took it for a strike, confident he'd timed Gordon, but he didn't see any more fastballs. Gordon followed the fastball with a series of curveballs, each one nastier than the last. "Those were three of the best pitches I'd ever seen," he said. He learned his lesson when it came to pinch hitting. "These guys have out pitches, so be aggressive from the beginning. Don't let a fastball go."

Mark, Adam's father, beamed with pride. "Adam didn't have an easy ride through college or the minor leagues by any means," he commented. "In college he battled through some depression to get back up. From the weight room injuries to his leg getting mangled sliding into home plate over a baseball bat, he struggled at times to get back up, but he did." Here was his son in a Chicago Cubs uniform. He was officially a major leaguer.

"We ran down to get pictures," Wendy said. She watched her son as he walked toward the batter's box. "He looked so calm." Loren called Keri on her cell phone. Max and Sam watched intently from the seats near home plate. Adam dreamed it and worked harder than anyone they'd ever known to make it real. Now he was doing it.

De Los Santos stepped on the rubber and peered toward the catcher for the sign. Adam would have three tenths of a second to react to whatever he threw. During his first nationally televised plate appearance, he didn't want to embarrass himself by bailing out on a Tom Gordon-esque curveball. Adam told himself to "lock and load," stay through the ball, and attack through the middle. *You're on ESPN right now so stay in there*, he told himself.

De Los Santos nodded, started his windup, and released the baseball. Adam was locked in, trying to pick up the rotation as soon as it left his hand. He heard the ball hissing right at him. He stood his ground, but it didn't break toward the plate like Gordon's curveballs. It kept coming, straight at his head. He attempted to turn away, but it was too late. The baseball struck Adam on the right side of his head, just under the base of the helmet. The sound was awful.

My head exploded with pain. I heard the impact, then nothing else. My eyes rolled into the back of my head. I thought I was about to die. I went to the ground, grabbing my head with both my hands. I literally thought I was holding my head together. My batting gloves felt soaked. I thought they were covered in blood. I began to chant to myself 'stay alive, stay alive, stay alive.' It was the scariest moment of my life.

Valerio De Los Santos thought he'd killed Adam. Who could survive being hit directly in the head with a 92 mile-an-hour fastball? He wandered aimlessly on the grass in front of the pitcher's mound as Adam writhed in agony inside the batter's box. De Los Santos appeared dazed as trainers bolted onto the field. The Marlins catcher Paul Lo Duca threw off his mask and immediately hovered over Adam. He patted his chest and side telling him, "Stay down, man. You're going to be okay." Adam's panic began to retreat when he realized Lo Duca wasn't screaming for a medic or telling anyone to get towels. Adam thought they would need towels for all the blood. If he was holding his skull together, wouldn't they need towels for that? He started to realize he wasn't bleeding although he could feel massive swelling setting in.

"The sound was terrible," Wendy recalled. Her world began to spin. Usually when Adam had an injury of some kind he would give her a hand sign that he was good, that he was okay. She didn't get one. Dusty and the team surrounded him. Mark was at her side. Anxiety flared within her. Mark O'Neal, the Cubs trainer, raced toward Adam and began to assess the extent of damage. He asked questions like "How many fingers am I holding up?" He told Adam to follow his finger with his eyes. As Adam began to breathe and recover, O'Neal asked Adam where he was two days ago. He answered without hesitating, "In the minor leagues and I'm not going back!" Adam's voice cut the tension of the moment. Everyone laughed nervously as they walked him back to the dugout. "He's good," someone said.

Adam sat down in the dugout. Someone handed him an ice pack. He was embarrassed, frustrated. This was his first plate appearance in the majors? He seemed okay, so he wasn't sent to the hospital. It was years before concussion protocols. Carlos Zambrano was ordered in to pinch run. Adam stared at first base, gleaming in the ball park lights. It felt miles away. He couldn't wait to get back. There were a thousand firsts still waiting for him. He would only have to wait a night or two more, and he'd be living his dream. He was a Major League Baseball player. "My heart sank when he got hit. The pitcher was remorseful. Adam's mom and dad came into the clubhouse," Dusty said. "It was one of the saddest days I've experienced in baseball."

In Adam's Own Words...

You and I will face difficult times in our lives. That's guaranteed. Pain can be sudden and devastating, or it can be slow and persistent. It hurts when I fail, lose someone, or have something valuable taken away. At the time, I usually don't understand why. But when we are blindsided by pain, confusion, and desperation, it's not something to fear. It's an opportunity to become wiser, stronger, more connected, and more powerful. It's an opportunity to persevere.

We have a choice to make. We can feel sorry for ourselves and blame others or the circumstances. If that's what we choose, we'll cement ourselves into a continuous cycle of pain and never grow beyond it. If we suppress our emotions entirely or drown ourselves in them, we'll find ourselves immobilized. We will be prevented from finding the true gift inside the troubles we face.

- Adam

Part 2 | Chasing a Dream

How to Tie Your Shoes

After the game, Adam and his family went back to the hotel. He stared at the wall, watching the minutes drag across the clock. Mark flipped through the same magazine he'd read three times already and yawned. Wendy brought another ice pack. So much for his first plate appearance in the majors. Adam turned off the TV. He didn't feel like watching himself getting hit by the pitch again. All the light in the room was giving him a nasty headache anyway. The darkness was comforting.

His first plate appearance was over. There was nothing he could do to change it. He pushed it out of his mind and tried to focus on the next one. He knew he needed to focus on what he could control. Who was next on the schedule? How were their starting pitchers? How was their bullpen? Who would serve up his first hit? Adam sat up as the adrenaline began to flow but winced. The jolt of pain that shot from his head to his waist told him to stay still. *All right, all right*, he thought. He would let his body recover first.

Adam told himself this was just another setback. He'd almost lost two of his fingers on his right hand and came back stronger. He'd already overcome a surgically repaired left wrist and won. He even beat a life-threatening infection in his leg that bled so much internally it turned his leg black. He was a member of the Chicago Cubs. He was in the major leagues and his lifelong dream came true. He was facing another terrifying and excruciating experience, but it was not going to stop him.

The next day Adam returned to the stadium and slowly pulled on his uniform. The major league socks were amazing. He paused with pleasure at seeing his name on the back of his jersey before sliding it over his sore neck and shoulder. He finished suiting up and walked through the tunnel toward the field. Adam quickly reached for his sunglasses as he walked into the intensifying light. The light pounded his eyes until his brain throbbed with pain. A wave of nausea hammered his gut and swelled into his esophagus. He squinted and ran his hand along the bench until he found a place to sit. "You good, man?" someone asked. "Yeah, I'm good," Adam said, fighting it. *Keep going, you're a big leaguer now*, he told himself.

Adam continued to fight his concussion symptoms throughout the game from the dugout. He squinted through his sunglasses and sometimes closed his eyes altogether just to give himself relief from the merciless glaring light. He nodded off sitting up. His chin dipped and a burst of neck pain jolted him awake. Adam sat on the bench, trying to be alert. His mind began to run wild. He felt a brief flicker of fear. *What's wrong with me? I'm sitting in a major league dugout finally, and I can barely stay awake?*

After the game, Adam took himself to a local hospital to be evaluated. Something wasn't right. Imaging and scans revealed no skull fractures or common brain injuries. The visit to the local hospital didn't provide any clues. The discharge documentation just read: Concussion. Adam tried to think positive about it. He extinguished the fear. *There's bound to be some pain like this afterward. I just need some time to recover*, he thought. At night, Adam slept upright because laying down was agonizing. He propped himself up to prevent nausea and persistent headaches. Day by day he waited for the symptoms to subside. Every second was a reminder of that pitch. The most phenomenal moment of his entire life had become his greatest agony in just three tenths of a second.

Keith Miller described seeing Adam get hit in the head as "one of the scariest things I'd ever seen. I was attached, and there was a fondness for him. It was one of the worst feelings possible to see that happen." At that time, there was little awareness about the effects of concussions in baseball. "I don't think at the time we fully knew what was going on. At times, he was symptom free. We were trying to get him right," he said. "We know so much more about concussions now. It's not even close to what it was then."

Precious *months* later, Adam would come to a sobering understanding that none of the performed evaluations or testing included a detailed assessment of the trauma to his inner ear or the affect it had on his vision. No one suspected or detected calcium carbonate crystals were blasted from the gel in Adam's inner ear labyrinth into one or more of the fluid-filled semicircular canals. If so, he would've been better prepared for what was happening to him. He would've known he may experience non-life threatening sudden spells where he felt he was caught in a rotational movement. Maybe he would have known that when his head moved a certain way or was in a particular position, it would trigger what's known as *Benign Paroxysmal Positional Vertigo.*

The All-Star break approached and Adam was relieved. It would give his body more time to heal. He headed back home to Connecticut to get some much-needed rest. Hopefully he would be ready after the break. It was good to be home, but he dreamed of returning to the Cubs clubhouse. He longed to wear the jersey and feel the Chicago cap on his head. He wanted to steal a base in every stadium in the major leagues. He wanted to snatch home run balls out of the air as they tried to escape from Wrigley Field over the outfield wall. He wanted to get the tip of the cap from a thankful pitcher for saving the game. He wanted everything he'd been dreaming of since he was a child.

Adam stared at the trim running along the bathroom wall adjacent to the floor tile. *What just happened?* He remembered walking into the bathroom, and now he was laid out on the floor. He'd blacked out. He was able to raise his arm. He reached out and touched the wall. Everything was spinning. The fear he thought he'd drowned came gasping to the surface. There was something definitely wrong. Adam tried to remain calm. He tried to get up.

His eyes shifted from side to side against his will. Adam couldn't control his own eyes! *What was going on? This wasn't just a concussion. There was more to this.* He couldn't bend over to tie his shoes without reeling from headaches that persisted for hours afterward. Adam's heart began to pound through his chest. He wondered when it would happen next. *When he was standing in the outfield? When he was driving? When he was at the grocery store?* Dizziness and pain overtook him. He was used to being strong, driven, athletic and confident in his movements. Now he felt vulnerable and unsteady. He braced himself and tried to stand back up without falling.

The All-Star break ended, and Adam was on an airplane back to Chicago. He forced himself to take batting practice on the field. His eyes felt detached, like they were floating through the air. He struggled to see the ball clearly and steadied himself during dizzy spells. He attempted to run, but he couldn't find the ground with his feet. Nothing felt right. Everything he was accustomed to performing at a world class level became foreign and awkward. The media asked Adam how he was feeling. Fighting to get well and stay put, he grappled with what to say. He told media members he felt "a little cloudy" and left it at that. He knew it was more than that, but this was his shot to remain here. He wasn't going back! He willed his body into order. He begged his body to be trustworthy again.

Adam remained with the Cubs through four more games as the team battled the Pittsburgh Pirates. He spent his free time calling doctors, asking questions, and frantically searching for answers about what was happening to him. If he was going to stay in the major leagues, he needed to provide the spark the Cubs expected from him. Yet he continued to find himself immersed in an unfamiliar darkness. He felt it coming.

He hung up the phone as another doctor's office remained puzzled over his symptoms and promised a call back in a week or two. Adam didn't have a week or two. The business of baseball must go on. The Cubs general manager called Adam in for private meeting. He said they were going to send him to their spring training facilities in Arizona to get well. He advised that's where they have medical staff year-round that could help him. The message was clear. The recent congratulatory excitement of being welcomed onto the Cubs was being replaced by the contradictory message that Adam was unworthy to continue in their ranks.

He stared at the Chicago Cubs jersey with his name hanging in his locker. He endured the silence of the players around him as he packed his things. A sense of shame whirled around him. His dream, which created so much achievement and pride in his life, suddenly peppered him with embarrassment. He wondered if this was all some sort of cruel joke reality was playing on him. Adam returned to his hotel. The light of the clubhouse, the locker room, the stadium, the fans, and the game he loved felt darker. Nauseous, he filled his travel bag and zipped it shut. It was no longer empty. It was heavy and full. Adam was going back down. He'd lasted 21 days in the big leagues. He saw one pitch and never took the field. Fighting back against the sting, Adam tried to focus on getting back, on what he could control. He fought through everything else he faced. He'd been counted out before. He encouraged himself. He told himself he'd get up again.

Adam arrived in Arizona and met with the team doctors. They applied a neck brace and said if he was symptom free for 72 hours he could take it off. Adam slept sitting up in a chair and endured the next three days until they took off the brace. They told him to touch his toes. He did, and this time he didn't black out. The training staff told Adam if he was in good enough condition to complete a few sprints that he could get back at it. That day he was able to sprint without difficulty. He hoped his symptoms were officially buried. Adam waited for the call to get sent back up the major leagues. He was good.

Adam's phone rang. It was the Cubs farm director who informed him that he'd been optioned down to the Double-A West Tennessee Jaxx. It stung, and Adam was frustrated. This was not the call he was expecting. He prepared to play again in the minor leagues and met up with the team during a road trip. In his first game back, he went 1 for 4 at the plate, but felt heavy on his feet after all of the time off to recover. After an 8-hour bus ride back home, they arrived in Jackson, Tennessee. He slept lying down that night without any problems but woke in the morning to the sound of his phone ringing. As he sat up and reached for the phone, all the symptoms flooded back. His eyes moved uncontrollably, pain from a severe headache split his skull, and nausea rippled through his abdomen. Adam tried to steady himself and fight back the pain. He called the team trainer, who picked him up and brought him to the hospital, but they could not provide any relief.

For the rest of the year Adam dealt with being blind-sided by these debilitating symptoms seemingly at random. Some days he was fine. Other days he was shaken by the sudden surfacing of dizziness, uncontrolled eye movements, balance problems, and headaches. A leader of the organization openly accused Adam of faking his symptoms in front of his teammates. He fought back the shame and anger of having an internal injury that couldn't be clearly seen or easily fixed. Adam never made excuses in his entire life, and now he was being accused of not only making excuses but inventing his symptoms? Soon after, he was informed he would not be an everyday player in Double-A.

Raw with frustration, Adam asked for a release from his contract. Because of positive relationships he'd built with others in the organization, they agreed to let him out. Again, he filled his travel bag and walked out of the clubhouse. The door closed silently behind him. He walked into the world disoriented and without a team. A time and place he loved had died.

The Cubs organization had been the gateway to his highest professional achievement. It was familiar, sacred, and a source of pride. It was ripped away from him. Adam reeled at how cruel life could be. Regardless of whether anyone understood it, he realized he was facing a challenge larger than just playing the game. His challenge was to understand what exactly happened to him and how he could heal from it. Baseball, which monopolized Adam's consciousness for his entire life, now took a seat in the dugout and sat the bench.

Health and wellness became what mattered most. Compounding his desperation was the realization that a disreputable realtor had taken advantage of Adam in a real estate business deal. He was stuck with an enormous mortgage for not one, but two homes he couldn't sell because of a loss in value. His savings were evaporating. Trying desperately to overcome this financial difficulty, Adam invested heavily into a developing social media startup. As he fought through the headaches and stress, Adam watched a company owned by one person make a series of vital mistakes and eventually lose it all.

Each moment without a headache became a gift. Every foot step he took that felt properly connected with the ground comforted him. Moments free of dizziness and sensitivity to light wrapped Adam in a feeling of serenity he sought to make permanent. Struggles he never saw coming continued to wallop him, but he was facing them head-on with every ounce of strength and tenacity he possessed. The battle Adam fought for the decade prior was on a baseball field, but the battle confronting him now was within his own body and mind. He was down now, writhing in confusion and questions. He was tempted by self-pity and shame, but he refused to give up. Adam, tenacious as always, refused to be defeated. There was more than just a professional baseball career at stake. He was going to do everything in his power to get back up.

In Adam's Own Words…

There is so much value in having a more experienced voice available while you pursue your goals. An example of this is when my father warned me not to invest in the startup that I was excited about early in my playing career. He advised me that people are often more important than the idea. He taught me that it doesn't matter how great the idea is, it will likely fail if you don't have an experienced team to execute. I chose to forge ahead with the investment anyway but lo and behold, he was right. At the very least, relying on him helped me minimize the mistake, and I gained invaluable experience through his insight.

– Adam

I'm Going to Get Back

When the Dodgers made Adam an offer in 2006, he took it without hesitation. A new organization and a new environment was just what he needed to start his victorious comeback. Members of the media began making direct comparisons between Adam and Archibald "Moonlight" Graham, a former professional baseball player popularized by the film *Field of Dreams*. Neither had an opportunity to get an official major league at-bat. They both played baseball at the University of North Carolina at Chapel Hill. They even shared the same initials – AG. *Not so fast, I'm not done yet*, Adam thought to himself. The comparisons felt like someone was trying to put a shirt on him that didn't fit.

Adam earned another victory when it came to his health during the year. A physician from Connecticut accurately diagnosed him over the phone with *Benign Paroxysmal Positional Vertigo*. He listened intently to the first physician who pinpointed exactly what he had been experiencing and why. Finally, an answer. Peace, like rising waters, began to drown the panic associated with the sudden, blindsiding symptoms he still faced.

The physician described what the diagnosis meant for Adam and what he could expect as a result. A series of repositioning movements were prescribed, called the Epley Maneuver, designed to help move the small calcium crystals in his inner ear that had been displaced back into their proper position. Adam's symptoms suddenly weren't such an intimidating mystery. Their weaknesses were exposed and now, he had their number. The flaring fear he felt was extinguished in one liberating conversation. In seconds, an opponent which had made him feel powerless for the last year, had vanished.

Adam hung up the phone, leaned back, and closed his eyes. The gleaming white first base he never touched, felt closer. His dream was no longer going to slip away. If his arm had been broken, everyone would've *seen* it and given him time to heal before reinstating him. Since no one saw the dislodged calcium crystals in his inner ear, his symptoms had been a troubling mystery to both Adam and the baseball organizations he'd spent all his energy trying to impress.

Although he would later learn his vision had been seriously affected as well, he still earned an on-base percentage of .387 during the season by earning more walks than hits. His batting average was a respectable .228 given his symptoms, while hitting .455 against lefties and .313 with runners in scoring position. Sadly, it wasn't enough. The Dodgers chose not to re-sign him at the end of the season.

Upon hearing the news, Adam walked toward one of the practice fields and found a quiet spot. The bat leaned on his neck as he stepped onto the brilliant emerald green grass. It had been over a year since he almost died on a field like this. He squatted down and ran his hand through the dirt. The terror of that moment flashed through his mind. *Stay alive, stay alive, stay alive* he told himself, convinced he was holding pieces of his head together. He'd been holding the pieces together for a long time. Was all this work still worth it?

A warm breeze blew toward the infield from center, blanketing him like the ocean breeze that had surrounded him in Miami. He didn't understand. He thought of his family and how much he loved them. He knew his pain hurt them too as they watched him endure his comeback. He knew those close to him must secretly wonder if his insatiable drive to play baseball had become a tortured obsession. He had a good run and achieved a plate appearance in the major leagues. It was a cruel narrative, but maybe that was his story. Maybe that was his legacy in baseball. *If it was time to walk away, what could possibly replace my love for this game*, Adam wondered.

He stood up and sighed, his mind traveling back to that fateful first pitch and the raw emotion of getting released by the Cubs. He thought of his dwindling bank account, the two mortgages he was paying, and his frustration for allowing himself to partner with a disreputable person who didn't hesitate to put him in this position for their own gain. Adam looked down at the baseball in his hand and ran his finger over the smooth leather cover with stitching as red as his surgical scars. Anyone who loved the game of baseball knew that an at-bat was never just about getting a hit. Regardless of the pain and struggle, Adam decided he was not done. There was more in store.

Following his release by the Dodgers, the Kansas City Royals contacted Adam. The past was gone and the Royals organization wanted to give him an opportunity of a fresh start for the 2007 season. Adam took them up on the offer and soon arrived for spring training in Arizona where he was quickly introduced to Dr. Barry Seiller by a member of the training staff.

Dr. Seiller is an Ophthalmologist and founder of the Visual Fitness Institute in Vernon Hills, Illinois. After conducting extensive research into how an athletes' eyes can be trained to improve, he created a software program called the Vizual Edge Performance Trainer. Vizual Edge has been used by elite athletes, Olympic teams, professional sports teams, and collegiate teams all over the world. Dr. Seiller was working with the Royals to improve player performance through the strengthening of their vision. Since clients of the program also included those who suffered traumatic brain injury, he was eager to begin working with Adam to learn about his persistent post-concussion symptoms.

Dr. Seiller initially assessed Adam and found that "Adam had developed a common problem after an acute concussion called nystagmus. This means the patient has an inability to control their eye movements. Their fixation ability becomes compromised. When this happens, the patient experiences dizziness, nausea, and motion sickness. Common symptoms can also include amnesia and light sensitivity. The acute phase is usually one to two weeks. The subacute phase can last one to four weeks. The chronic phase can last for years."

When Dr. Seiller learned that Adam hit .228 in the Dodgers minor league system prior to treatment, he found it remarkable. "People with these symptoms often can't function in activities of daily living, let alone hit a baseball. It's dangerous for them to drive. They get overwhelmed by stimuli coming from every direction." To have such a batting average while dealing with nystagmus was "absolutely impressive." After Adam was hit, he experienced his eyes rolling backward, shifting of his eyes from side to side involuntarily, having an inability to control his eyes, light sensitivity, and feeling like his eyes were detached and floating in the air. "Because of these erratic eye movements, it creates difficulty with depth perception and any precise action of the eyes," Dr. Seiller said.

"There is a frequent visual component to concussions," Dr. Seiller continued, noting that medical providers who treat concussions often do not have a detailed understanding of vision or the associated vision problems which can result. It was common for him to see patients who had been to "seven or eight doctors" before finally being diagnosed effectively. Because of this, "patients are often discouraged and can become very depressed." It becomes empowering to the patient to finally understand what is wrong and how they can work to correct their problems instead of being isolated and feeling like no one understands.

Dr. Seiller quickly generated a treatment plan using his software which would help to strengthen Adam's eyes to correct the effects of being hit. The sense of powerlessness he felt as a result of the uncontrollable eye movements and vision changes began to melt away. Reinvigorated, Adam relentlessly performed the eye exercises provided to him and frequently performed the prescribed Epley Maneuver. After a successful spring training, he felt a renewed sense of confidence. His batting average jumped to .266 and he began hitting for the most power of his career with the Double-A Wichita Wranglers. His on-base percentage rose to .373 which ranked tenth in the league. He led the league with 11 triples and ranked second with 13 sacrifice hits. He ranked fourth in the league with 74 walks and earned 23 stolen bases. He led his team by scoring 73 runs.

Dr. Seiller hopes those who learn about Adam's story will know how important it is not to give up. To persevere through post-concussion symptoms while competing at such a high level was "extraordinary" in his opinion. Adam could've easily given up after seeing numerous doctors who didn't validate or identify the link between the visual impairments and the trauma of getting struck in the head. He didn't. He got up, kept going and found the answers he needed to propel him forward.

In Adam's Own Words...

What I have learned is not to run away from pain. We must find a way to learn from it and resolve it, so that we can overcome it. Otherwise the problem will only continue, decreasing the chances day-by-day that we will be able to persevere through it. We'll encounter the same problem again and again until we choose to analyze the source and understand what created it. Once we understand the cause, and create a solution, we're freed up to move on to the next challenge. Our fear and anxiety decreases significantly, and we begin to feel a sense of empowerment. We may even start to look forward to the next challenge.

– Adam

Not a One Pitch Guy

Adam re-signed with the Kansas City Royals for the 2008 season, and the last day of training camp finally arrived. The team buses were loaded with equipment and ready to head out to their minor league destinations to start the season. Adam's performance was solid during spring training, and he was confident it was worthy of a Triple-A roster spot. The problem was he'd already been told they didn't have room for him in Triple-A Omaha. Instead he would be sent to Double-A in Arkansas. *Either way, at least it was a place to play*, Adam told himself.

He left his house at the usual time of 3:30 a.m. His bags were packed, and he was ready for the one-hour commute to the Royals spring training facility in Surprise, Arizona. He loaded his bags on the bus headed for Double-A and walked into the clubhouse to change. After getting dressed for his final on-field workout, one of the front office staff asked Adam to come upstairs. He thought nothing of it. If anything, he allowed a bit of excitement to set in, pondering what this could mean. Maybe a Triple-A roster spot freed up for him? Maybe he was heading to Omaha after all, just one step away from the majors.

Adam sat down in the office. "We're going in a different direction," they told him. "We're releasing you." Adam wasn't going to Triple-A Omaha. He wasn't going to Double-A Arkansas either. He was going nowhere. He was flat broke, without a team, and responsible for two houses he could no longer afford. His world was collapsing. To make matters worse, his bags were already on the road to Arkansas. Adam asked the Royals to ship his bags back to him as soon as possible. They said they would, but they never did. Weeks later, his former hitting coach with the Royals, Tommy Gregg, finally tracked down his belongings and shipped them to Adam's parents in Guilford.

He didn't want to speak to anyone. He'd never felt lower. As depression began to set in, the phone rang from an unknown number. Adam didn't answer, and the caller left a voicemail. Hours later, he finally mustered enough curiosity to see who it was from. What he found was a message from Dusty Baker that Adam would treasure for the rest of his life. As he listened to Dusty, his depression and anxiety melted away. It was the most heartfelt message he ever received. Although the details will never be publicly shared, Adam drew solace and strength from Dusty's words which confirmed he was a good man and God had a plan for him. Dusty encouraged Adam to stay positive.

He called Dusty back. Their conversation took Adam by the heart and hand. It helped him out of the darkness of his depression. Negativity vanished. He knew his problems remained, but he'd regained enough strength to face them. He was able to banish depression, self-doubt, fear, anxiety, and self-pity when he squared off on himself in the mirror in Lansing, but he needed a friend to help him get up after being let go from the Royals.

Dusty helped Adam understand he needed to keep moving forward and never give up on his dream.

Something was in store for him. He would overcome his problems one step at a time. When Adam hung up the phone, he felt focused on his ultimate goal. He felt peace knowing it was not time to give up. He wouldn't quit. It was time to get back up and keep going.

Adam signed a contract with the Bridgeport Bluefish to play independent baseball near his home town. After performing well to start the season, the Anaheim Angels organization offered him a minor league contract with the Double-A Arkansas Travelers. He was immediately playing centerfield and leading off. Reinvigorated, he quickly established himself as the team leader by hitting over .330 during his first month with the team. Members of the front office pulled Adam aside in the clubhouse and said he was the current manager's type of player – hard-nosed and unafraid to grind out tough at-bats and create opportunities on the field. The organization wanted wins, and if Adam could consistently perform the way he began, he was told he would make it back to the major leagues. Again, his dream was right in front of him. His decision to keeping pushing forward was the right one and this validated it.

Being released by Kansas City was still fresh in Adam's mind. The Travelers were scheduled to play Kansas City's Double-A affiliate, the Northwest Arkansas Naturals, near the end of the first half of the season. Minor league seasons are played in two halves, divided by the All-Star break in July. Teams with the best record in the first half automatically make the postseason playoffs. The same is true for teams with the best record after the All-Star break. The Travelers were in the hunt to win the first half of the season.

The night before the game, the team assembled for a meeting. They would face a pitcher with the most dominant earned run average in the league. While reviewing the game plan in front of the team, the manager looked at Adam and said, "Greeny, you're the spark. When you get on base, we win." Always team oriented, he felt a slight discomfort at being mentioned above his peers but also felt good that the team trusted in him.

Adam carved his cleats into the batter's box to lead off the game. He scanned the field populated with players who were his teammates just a short time ago. He locked and loaded and waited for the pitcher's offering. He made solid contact, and the ball rifled toward the left field wall. Adam rounded first base and sprinted towards second. A cleanly fielded ball would hold him up there, but he was always hungry for an extra base.

The ball ricocheted off the bottom of the left field wall, and the outfielder scrambled to catch up to it. That was just the window of time Adam needed to stretch a double into a triple. He put his head down and accelerated towards third. Suddenly, he felt a pop followed by two more, and his right leg exploded with pain. Adam reached third safely as a tide of anger swelled within him. He knew he was hurt *again*. He ripped the helmet off his head and smashed it into the ground. He was relentless in taking care of his body before, during, and outside of the game. Still he found himself hobbling off the field.

He was sent for x-rays, but Adam knew the injury didn't involve the bone structures in his leg. He was diagnosed with a hamstring injury, but he didn't buy it. He asked for an MRI to understand what was really going on. The results of the MRI proved he was misdiagnosed. It was a ruptured Baker's Cyst instead. The treatment regimen involved rest and elevation for several weeks while fluid reabsorbed into his body, but Adam didn't have that long. The Travelers were going to face the first-place team in the league in *one* week. If they were going to lock up their postseason bid, they needed to win. They needed to win *now*.

Adam was given a few days off before the coaching staff approached him. Their back was against the wall. They had to win one of the next two games in order to ensure they made the playoffs. "You at 70 percent is still better than our other options. We need you," the coaches urged. The training staff said he couldn't re-injure the ruptured cyst, so he put the team first and agreed to play through the injury.

Adam winced at his performance. For the first time in his life, he struggled defensively. When he was 100 percent, a ball hit anywhere near him in centerfield landed in his glove. With his reduced range, that was no longer the case. The explosive speed he relied on to get him around the bases was noticeably absent as well. Adam felt like a shell of himself, but he gave everything he had. The Travelers lost his first game back. They had one more chance before the break to clinch.

Adam was up to bat in the ninth inning and watched the left-handed relief pitcher warm up on the mound. It was the same reliever he'd faced the night before. Following a common approach in baseball, Adam typically took the first pitch if it was a breaking ball such as a slider, curve, or a changeup, opting to wait for a good fastball instead. He struck out after taking on a first pitch breaking ball from this same pitcher last night. He told himself he'd be ready for it if he tried it again.

The Travelers were down a run. His teammates were on second and third base. It was up to him, and it was now or never. Adam readied himself as the reliever released the pitch. The baseball rocketed off his bat. He smashed the ball over the right fielder's head, who didn't even have a chance to move as the ball hit the grass once and bounced over the wall for a ground-rule walk-off double. The game was over. They secured their spot in the playoffs. His leg throbbed in pain as his teammates mobbed him. He shoved them away from his leg as they celebrated.

Following the brief All-Star break, Adam continued to play through the injury at less than 100 percent. His batting average dropped. With the playoffs looming near the end of the season, he hustled down the first base line after putting a routine ground ball in play. Again, he felt something pop in his right leg as he lunged toward the bag.

This time it *was* his hamstring. His season was over. Adam played a total of 70 games for the Travelers during the 2008 season, batting .271 with an on-base percentage of .361. He stole 16 bases. Despite playing such a key role in getting them there, the Travelers headed to the playoffs without him. Adam was placed on the disabled list and sent to Arizona for an off-season rehab assignment.

At the end of the year, the Angel's farm director and manager sat down with Adam. They were concerned about his consistency. He excelled during the first half of the season but hadn't maintained the same pace during the second. He tried to explain he was 100 percent healthy during the first half which allowed him to play to his full potential. He reminded them he was asked to return to the lineup knowing he wasn't completely healthy. Even while injured, it was his performance that earned the team a spot in the playoffs.

Adam's words weren't enough. He couldn't convince them to give him time to get healthy. Baseball is a business, and it's what a player has done lately that is most remembered. He'd left the nest of the first organization that invested so much in him. Now he was expendable. He didn't get an offer from the Anaheim Angels for the following spring. He again became a free agent and headed home to Guilford.

Lindsay Marottoli also grew up in Guilford. Adam was a grade ahead of her in school, and they quickly became friends. After graduation, both left their home town for college. Lindsay graduated from Assumption College with honors, triple majoring in English, Television and Theater Art, and Business Management. Besides being a dedicated student, she was always a die-hard Yankees fan.

Lindsay was a twin. Her sister Melissa was her best and closest friend. They were college roommates, worked together, and even bought their first home together. They'd never been apart longer than a week. Baseball was an escape for them, and they loved going to Yankees games or watching them on TV.

On November 11, 2007, Melissa was diagnosed with Stage IV lung cancer. The average life expectancy for a similar diagnosis is usually one year. She was just 26 years old. The word *incurable* attempted to intimidate a family built upon core values of faith, hope, life, and love. They were not going to be intimidated. They dug in and prepared to fight.

Adam had learned of Melissa's illness while playing with the Wichita Wranglers in Kansas during the prior season and had reached out to wish her well as she began her battle. After he arrived home, she was with her mother at Adam's parents' house for a visit where he learned more about her condition. A week later Melissa's mother was again at the Greenberg house, but this time Lindsay accompanied her as Melissa was not feeling well and stayed home. After talking for a few minutes, it dawned on Adam that it wasn't Melissa standing in front of him, but her twin Lindsay. As they began to reconnect, there was a spark.

Adam asked Lindsay if she wanted to go out that night. They began to date and were soon engaged to be married.

As Adam and Lindsay grew closer, he joined the Marottoli battle against cancer. Adam was impressed by Lindsay's relentless bravery and supported her as she tirelessly worked to save her sister. The Marottoli family reeled with questions as they attempted to cope with Melissa's diagnosis of lung cancer. She didn't smoke tobacco. How could she get lung cancer? She was too young. Why her? Why now?

Determined to find a cure, the Marottoli family sought answers, educated themselves on the disease, poured over research, and conducted their own. They requested the doctors not disclose any prognosis information to them in order to maintain positivity and faith. They refused to limit themselves to traditional medicine. They identified innovators and thinkers who were going above and beyond in cancer treatment and research in hopes of partnering with them to cure Melissa. Nothing would stop them.

Lindsay grappled with guilt and questions. Why not her? Why her sister? What transplant could be performed? What intervention? They shared the same DNA. They were twins. What part of her could be sacrificed to save her sister and best friend? Questions and emotions battered her as she sought to cope with the trauma of slowly losing her twin sister. She relied upon Adam. He was her "backbone" Lindsay said. "I can drown in my grief. Adam gets me out of drowning mode and helps to keep me in the fight. Together, we keep the fight going."

In Adam's Own Words...

We're human, which means we're susceptible to letting each other down, typically without even knowing it. It also means we're capable of choice, the choice to consciously pick each other up without asking for anything in return. Simply because it's the right thing to do. Simply because we're all in this together. Trust that it is always what you choose to do next that can carve out your journey.

As I look back on my journey, our journey, I just can't imagine what things would have been like if I hadn't had teammates, coaches, and family around me to pick me up when moving forward seemed far from possible. They helped me refocus, stay positive, and push forward. Trust in those who are willing to pick you up, even during your darkest days. If you work hard, have the right attitude, do right by those close to you, they will be there to help and assist when you need it most.

– Adam

"God Has a Plan"

Dusty Baker had become the manager of the Cincinnati Reds organization, and he personally invited Adam to sign a minor league contract with the Reds to come to spring training to start the 2009 season. He jumped at the opportunity. The only major league manager Adam had ever known, who'd given him the nod for his first and only plate appearance in Chicago so many years ago, was validating all the effort he put into his health and baseball. Taking the time to understand his symptoms, shed toxic environments, identify a course of action to repair his vision, and persevere through the confusion and frustration paid off. Dusty knew what type of player Adam was and what he could be at the highest level.

Adam was the fastest player in camp. The Reds staff knew he was quick but didn't expect this level of performance. Adam's dominance earned statements from legends like Dusty and others on the major league staff that if Adam kept performing like this, it was likely he was going to get called up that season. He could taste it. It was right there. This was his way back. Not only did he need it emotionally and spiritually, he needed the finances a major league salary would bring. He was buried in debt and contemplating filing for bankruptcy.

David Bell is the current bench coach for the Saint Louis Cardinals. He played professional baseball for 12 years. During his career, he batted in 589 runs, hit 123 home runs, and earned a lifetime batting average of .257. He played all four infield positions during the course of his career spanning the Cleveland Indians, Saint Louis Cardinals, Seattle Mariners, San Francisco Giants, Philadelphia Phillies, and the Milwaukee Brewers. As a coach, Bell worked for the Chicago Cubs prior to being hired by the Saint Louis Cardinals. He managed the Double-A Carolina Mudcats as well as the Triple-A Louisville Bats for the Cincinnati Reds. In 1994, Bell won the Lou Boudreau Award. In 2002, he won the Willie Mac Award for spirit and leadership. On June 28, 2004, he hit for the cycle and joined his grandfather, Gus Bell, as the first grandfather and grandson duo to achieve this feat in Major League Baseball history. Outside of the Bell family, there are only four other families that earned the honor of having three generations play Major League Baseball.

Spring training was the first time David met Adam when he was managing the Carolina Mudcats for the Reds. "Adam had already played for my father in Kansas City. I knew my dad loved him. He was well-respected and well-liked. My first impression of Adam was how smart he was. His intelligence on the field carried over to how he conducted himself off the field. He was a hard worker. He was driven. He was a good teammate."

"I really appreciated Adam's approach to the game," Bell said. "He went out of his way to make the team better while he was working hard personally to get back to the majors. It was clear to me that he was going to be successful no matter what he did because of how he went about it. He was doing things the right way. When a manager has players like Adam, it makes the job easy. With all the different personalities we typically have to deal with, that's not always the case."

Bell described the impact Adam made during camp. "When I won the Willie Mac award in 2002, it was very personal for me. It was truly meaningful. The reason why it meant so much is because of what it represented and because my teammates voted on who should receive it. To have my teammates choose to give the award to me made it more special than other awards I received. It was on a whole other level because you can't fool your teammates. They are in it with you every day. Adam's teammates had that same type of respect for him. He didn't need to use words to lead. He set the example in what he did. If there was a Willie Mac award at Cincinnati when Adam was there, he would've won it."

Bell was transitioning from being a professional baseball player to a manager when he and Adam met. "I was a young manager when I met him, and Adam was very perceptive. Because he was so intelligent, his presence and example challenged me to be a better manager. I didn't want to let guys like him down. He was doing everything he could to help the team. Certainly, the expectation of the team is that the leader possesses the same commitment. I knew as a new manager that I was not going to fool anyone. When they were giving everything they had, I owed it to them to do the same."

As the best spring training of his life came to a close, there were some changes announced within the organization. Adam was told they wanted to see him upstairs. He maintained his confidence. *There's no way I'm getting released*, Adam thought to himself. Not after how well he had just performed. Another minor league player walked in, and ten seconds later, walked out. He told Adam as he walked by, "I got released." Adam's gut began to churn.

They called Adam in, and he sat down. The room was silent. They shut the door, and no one spoke. Adam didn't know it yet, but the business of baseball was about to deal yet another crushing blow, one he hadn't see coming. Finally, one of the coaches said, "Well, I guess I'll start this." He explained that all the other major league outfielders had picked up their assignments. For Adam to have a spot with the Reds, one of them would've needed to decline. Adam felt like he'd been hit by another errant fastball, this time straight to the chest. They offered him a coaching job. If he didn't take it, they were releasing him.

Adam's dream was to *play* Major League Baseball. He wasn't ready to be a coach. He knew he could play at that level. He felt the breeze of his lifelong dream slipping away. Dazed, Adam stood and wandered aimlessly out the door. The business of baseball was asking why he wouldn't go away, why he was still standing there, and how long could he persevere? How long could he sustain this fight? Was his love of the game worth this amount of pain?

Adam wandered toward Dusty's office. Thoughts and emotions swirled within him. Another coach explained to Dusty that Adam was being released. Recognizing all Adam had endured, Dusty paused for a moment and looked at this young man standing in his doorway. He knew how much of a warrior Adam was. He was nearly killed by the first pitch of his first major league plate appearance, and here he was *years* later still warring for a spot on a major league roster. He knew a million other men would've hung it up a long time ago.

Dusty saw the storm within Adam and could see he was barely holding on. "Adam, God has a plan for you. Go home. Do what you need to do for yourself and your family. But don't give up." Adam barely had the strength to lift his eyes toward the baseball icon in front of him. Dusty knew who Adam was, where he'd been, and what this meant. He was dying inside, but if Dusty still had faith, he could too.

Disoriented, Adam walked to the clubhouse, opened his locker, and stared at his belongings. His eyes burned and blurred with tears. He split open his duffle bag and began to fill it. Once the locker was a dark and empty tomb, Adam heaved the duffle bag over his shoulder. He pulled the piece of tape with his name written on it off the locker and tossed it in the garbage can. He stared at his name laying there in the trash until it blurred from the next round of welling tears. Adam tried to compose himself and walked out of the locker room.

Adam said his goodbyes to his teammates as they completed their last day of spring training without him. They were shocked to learn he had been cut from the team. His heart ached during the long walk past all the practice fields and into the parking lot, his duffle bag straps cutting into his shoulder. The sweet music of baseballs popping into leather gloves and rocketing off wooden bats in the cages slowly faded into the distance. His exhausted mind wondered how he could face Lindsay. He looked to the sky and glared into the brutal Florida sun. He had no money and no contract. His savings were gone, and he'd just declared bankruptcy. For the love of the game he'd given *everything*.

The waves of emotion receded. Yet again, he evaluated where he was and what he had control over. What could he do? Adam closed his eyes and decided he would go back and play for the Bridgeport Bluefish again. He picked up the phone to secure the job, then walked across the street to deliver the news to Lindsay who was waiting anxiously in the condo where they had been staying. Adam broke down in front of his soon-to-be wife and told her that he had been released. They were going back to Connecticut empty handed. "I wanted to give him another shot," Baker said, "but there just wasn't enough room on the roster."

In Adam's Own Words...

Attitude is a decision that we alone can control. No one else controls it for you unless you empower them do to so. When good or bad things happen, it's our choice to determine how we perceive it and ultimately handle it. Studies have repeatedly shown that the power of positive thought is real and exists within each one of us. It's up to you.

How do you harness this power when something affects your attitude? I've found many ways. Listen to music, take a walk, call a friend, follow positive people and accounts on social media, find something in that moment that makes you feel thankful. As tough as it may seem at the time, nothing overcomes a bad attitude like the feeling of gratefulness. Next time you're feeling good, take stock of why, and save it for later. What made you feel that way? The weather? The radio? Another person? An activity? A memory?

Yes, bad things happen to us that are beyond our control but you can affect the outcome. You literally have the power to convince yourself of what your attitude should be, which determines what your actions will be, which has ultimate control over the result. Every life-changing action, intervention or invention, no matter how small or big, begins with a thought. Always remember, no matter what happens – you are in control of your own attitude.

– Adam

"He's a Visionary"

Soon after Adam began playing for the Bluefish for the second time, an opposing batter hit a shot to centerfield. He sprinted and dove, fully outstretched to catch the ball. Pain exploded in his left shoulder as he hit the ground. Back in the dugout, he tried to cope with whatever had just gone wrong and attempted to swing a bat. He dropped it halfway through the swing as bolts of pain ransacked his arm and shoulder.

Adam fought to cope with the injury. He couldn't stand the thought of another surgery and more rehabilitation. His batting average dropped off as he altered his swing to compensate for the pain. He knew he was injured, but he couldn't stand another potential delay in getting back to the major leagues. Adam picked up the phone and called his friend Dr. Michael Lebowitz.

Dr. Lebowitz is a Chiropractic Doctor who has practiced applied kinesiology for more than 35 years. He has written four books, has published more than 60 articles, and developed healing techniques which are used throughout the United States, Canada, Europe, Asia, Africa, and Australia. He participates in the development of nutritional products and performs research for nutrition and nutraceutical companies. Dr. Lebowitz is also a fan and memorabilia collector of Jewish baseball players.

Back in 2003, Dr. Lebowitz brought his son to a spring training game in Mesa, Arizona, and approached Adam for an autograph. A friendship quickly developed. Adam was engaged by Dr. Lebowitz's expertise in nutrition and his unique insights into the relationship between nutrition and athletic performance. Their conversations often felt to Dr. Lebowitz as timely and "meant to be."

After Adam explained what had just happened with his shoulder, Dr. Lebowitz immediately recommended a whole food product called velvet deer antler, a staple of ancient Chinese medicine. "Velvet deer antler has all the constituents in it to help build cartilage, restore bone injuries, and repair parts of the body after injury. It is also helpful with autoimmune diseases where the human body attacks itself. When you ingest something that is similar to a part of your body, it can help fool it into attacking the substance instead," Dr. Lebowitz said.

Adam began to notice a difference within days. He became less sore and soon experienced increased flexibility and mobility. He didn't require as much time to warm-up. His muscles required less stretching, and his legs felt fresher. Adam didn't receive any cortisone shots or anti-inflammatory pain medication and credited his improvements to the velvet deer antler. Dr. Lebowitz "knew it worked from clinical research, but it surprised me how well it worked for him."

For the next four and a half months, Adam played every game, fighting through the pain in his shoulder. He focused on stealing bases as a way of contributing to the team. He stole 55 of them that season, enduring the blast of pain and numbness following every slide into a base. As the season came to a close, Adam approached the team physician, Dr. Kwok, and confessed he'd been playing with an injury the entire year.

Dr. Patrick Kwok, M.D. is a board certified orthopedic surgeon who served as the team doctor for the Bluefish. He performed some physical tests on Adam's shoulder, sent him for an MRI for further evaluation, and told him he would call as soon as the results came in. When his phone rang several days later, Adam was at the Dana Farber Cancer Institute in Boston with Lindsay and the Marottoli family. Not only did they just learn from Melissa's oncologist that her cancer was growing, Dr. Kwok had more bad news.

When Adam dove in the outfield, Kwok explained it resulted in a subluxation of his ball shoulder joint. This was not a full dislocation, but it was severe enough that the MRI proved his labrum was torn along with a 90 percent tear of his rotator cuff. He marveled at how Adam managed to play an entire season with such a painful injury. Although it would've been extremely difficult to hide if it was his throwing shoulder, Adam was able to keep the injury to himself due to its existence in his non-throwing arm, according to Kwok. Adam further credited the velvet deer antler and added he'd also been sticking to a regimented non-inflammatory diet at Dr. Leibowitz's guidance.

Dr. Kwok was skeptical and began researching

whether Adam was taking something harmful. There was very little research available in the United States about velvet deer antler but he recalled being able to locate a few peer reviewed articles about the product. He began to provide it to his colleagues who noticed a positive difference over the next few months. He also reached out to an associate in China who ensured him it was not harmful and had been used safely by people for more than 2,000 years.

Once he was satisfied it was safe, he conducted a test study on 100 of his post-surgical patients who were open to exploring pain relieving treatment modalities beyond non-steroidal medications, steroid injections, and narcotics. He tracked their experience with surveys and follow-up calls. No side effects were reported. Rather, many of his patients expressed that they valued the product and how effective it was for them. They noticed less joint pain, were getting looser quicker, and were experiencing less muscle ache and overall faster recovery. Adam's family, friends, and close teammates experienced similar results. It even appeared to help Adam's family dog move around better.

The rest of Adam's teammates began to take notice. They described feeling improvement of nagging or chronic injuries within days. Word spread even to opposing teams, as players hoped to find similar relief. Recognizing how effective it was in helping baseball players and post-operative surgical patients, the entrepreneur in Adam began stirring. "He was so impressed by the results that we decided to make it more widely available. I put him in touch with a supplier, and I served as a research advisor," Dr. Lebowitz said.

Adam worked with Dr. Kwok and Dr. Lebowitz, as well as former professional baseball player Danny Putnam and others to create a company called Lurong Living. According to Adam, "Lurong Living was founded on the core values of family, respect, honesty, hard work, trust, and the rejection of mediocrity. We believe that success isn't merely a result of treating others right, but it's established on a foundation of building others up. We believe our businesses' success is the vehicle to help change more lives on a daily basis in a positive way. These values shape our daily business, our innovations, our products, and how we engage the world."

Dr. Lebowitz's nutrition expertise certainly helped Adam physically, but he has "always been impressed by his optimism. Despite the adversity he experienced, he was willing to do whatever he needed to do to overcome it. What's amazing about him is that he views the whole picture when he views adversity. Many of us don't have the mindset to do that. He's a visionary."

Adam moved forward with the surgery to repair his shoulder. Dr. Kwok described a possible recovery time of between eight and twelve months. Adam knew the next baseball season started in five. After the surgery, he ran his fingertips across the fresh surgical site and told himself that anything over five months was not an option. He was going to be in uniform on opening day.

As Adam's shoulder healed, he rehabbed while focusing on his new business. He took a step back and focused on his overall health instead of allowing baseball to monopolize his mind and energy. "Adam has a unique story. He uses his experiences to connect with people. Everything that has happened to him he's turned into a positive. Lurong Living is just one part of that," admired Dr. Kwok. Adam assembled a team of people he knew he could trust who worked together to launch the Lurong Living brand. He enjoyed reaching beyond baseball to impact the wellness of others. Their stories and inspiration helped balance Adam and Lindsay as they supported Melissa's battle against cancer.

On October 16, 2010, Adam and Lindsay were married. Their honeymoon consisted of the first eight consecutive days Lindsay would ever be away from her sister. A month into their marriage, Lindsay boarded an airplane to Europe with her father Sal to gather information on how to best help Melissa. They scoured Europe to connect with progressive doctors performing the most innovative cancer treatments who could give them more days, more minutes, and more memories together. They hustled and networked, seeking an answer that could give every family suffering from the effects of cancer hope for the eradication of the disease and all its pain. "Adam knew he was taking a backseat to my pursuit of a cure for Melissa which I admire about him. He supported me the whole way. He encouraged me to look beyond traditional medicine and seek out the most progressive treatments for Mel." Lindsay could not begin to express how much it meant to her, Melissa, and her family for Adam's support during the most trying time of their lives.

Based on their research, they began to wonder if Lindsay's cancer-free immune system could be used to help Melissa fight off cancer? Physicians at the Institute for Tumor Therapy in Duderstadt, Germany, and the Institute of Hyperthermia and Immunotherapy in Vienna, Austria, agreed to find out. Soon injections of 5 to 20 million of Lindsay's white blood cells and killer cells were regularly administered to Melissa while she and Lindsay lived in Austria and Germany for treatment. They began to transition the treatments back to the United States after locating a doctor who was willing to oversee the treatment plan in New York.

Dr. Gettinger of the Yale New Haven Hospital Smilow Cancer Center credited Lindsay and her family for this forward thinking when it came to cancer treatment because at the time "we really didn't think of immunotherapy or modulating the immune system to fight cancer, or at least not for lung cancer." Melissa's condition improved, although she was not cured. She continued to live in quiet defiance of common expectations and made the most of every moment she lived. Melissa, her family, and her physicians committed every resource they could to her treatment.

When Lindsay's grief over setbacks in Melissa's cancer

treatment became too much to bear, she would reach out to her husband. She described how Adam "helped to cushion" the trauma as they talked through it. He also encouraged her to link up with support groups that could intimately understand the complexities of survivor's guilt and the trauma which comes from losing a twin to cancer. Every time she got down, Adam helped her get up.

Lurong Living was a positive focus for Adam as 2010 came to a close. He was newly married and trying to support himself and his wife. Not only could the company potentially supply additional income, he enjoyed connecting with people who experienced significant improvements in their quality of life as a result. Kwok described how Adam took his pain from athletic injuries and created something that has benefitted so many. "He discovered something that helped him immensely and was determined to make it available to everyone." "It's what any good teammate would do," said Adam.

Opening day of the 2011 Bridgeport Bluefish season approached, and Adam willed himself to be ready in less than half the typical recovery time by hard work, proper nutrition, and velvet deer antler. There was chatter in the clubhouse. Valerio De Los Santos now played for the Long Island Ducks. Adam knew it and had been preparing for the day he would again face the pitcher who obliterated his major league career in an instant. Adam wouldn't have to wait long. The Bluefish were scheduled to play the Ducks in the very first game of the season.

In Adam's Own Words...

Proactively pursuing the things that you are passionate about is a great way to overcome the obstacles you may face in life. Think about it. We naturally tend to apply cognitive bias, or subjective reality, to everything we see or do. If we're passionate about something, and come across a roadblock or speedbump, we are more likely to find a way around or over it. If not, we are more likely to see obstacles as an excuse to give up.

Allow yourself to follow your passions. That's vision. Then truly allow yourself the time to develop that vision into reality. That's how you become a visionary, free to allow your mind to bring your dreams into focus without outside distraction. An interesting thing happens when you develop this vision, you become less reactive to the environment around you. If we're always in a reactive state, we will never allow our minds to grow and pursue what's important to us. Don't give away your time to anything and everyone without giving it to yourself.

– Adam

"Bittersweet" Redemption

Sam, who would later also play for the Bluefish, watched as his big brother visited with De Los Santos in the outfield prior to the game. He wondered what Adam was thinking and saying. Adam was relentlessly positive, and Sam never saw an ounce of negativity from him. He wondered how the presence of De Los Santos would affect him. When Adam got back to the clubhouse, he didn't say anything about his conversation. No one spoke to him, and Adam didn't say a word.

Adam cleared the clubhouse and made his way to the dugout. It was game time. The world was about to see what happened whenever he set a goal. He was laser focused. At that moment Adam wasn't merely a baseball player, he was a warrior sprinting up the beach in his personal battle of Normandy. De Los Santos, a reliever, got the call to pitch in the eighth inning. Adam readied himself. It was time.

He made his way to the on-deck circle and stared at the pitcher's mound. The silhouette that haunted him for years stood before him. He felt the air go humid. His mind flickered with images. He saw the bottle of Dom Perignon glistening in the Florida sunlight in the beachfront Marriott suite. He saw the note from Keith Miller sitting next to it, congratulating Adam on making it. The bag he'd only been able to empty once laid on the floor in fleeting defeat. Adam heard Dick Pole bark at him to get a bat. He heard the echo of Dusty's voice telling him "Go get 'em, kid."

As Adam walked to the batter's box he thought he saw Todd Hollandsworth shuffling toward the dugout after grounding out. He dug in and sensed Paul Lo Duca scanning his face from behind his catcher's mask, waiting to issue the sign. He felt the explosion of pain, the terror, and the chasing helplessness. Adam forced himself to look at the man on the pitcher's mound and fought to control his breathing. This was not 2005. This was 2011. He banished every fear and scanned the field for vulnerabilities in the defense, gaps where he could hit the ball. There would be no surprises here. That gleaming white first base bag was going to be his.

Valerio De Los Santos watched the man who he thought he'd killed six years ago carve his cleats into the batter's box. He remembered the pitch leaving his hand and the terrible sound it made ricocheting off Adam's head. He remembered seeing Adam writhing on the ground and being walked off the field. Valerio remembered his own sleepless nights as the pitch he threw haunted him. De Los Santos toed the rubber on the pitcher's mound, came set, and heaved a cutter toward home.

Adam could see every detail of the world between them, and they were the only two in it. He clenched the bat and watched the ball leave the pitcher's left hand as he picked up the rotation of the seams. Fear launched its final assault. He felt his entire body tighten as the cut fastball edged inside toward him. Adam clamped down on his breathing, conditioned for an impending jolt of massive pain. The ball retreated from its threatening course, cut back over the plate, and pounded the catcher's glove. "Strike!" the umpire shouted.

The umpire's voice perforated Adam's eardrums as his body and mind slowly allowed themselves to recognize he was not hurt, not writhing in pain, and not laying on the ground. He was upright and armed. Adrenaline raided his bloodstream. He stepped out of the batter's box, waved the bat to loosen his clenched muscles, and began to breathe again. Adam looked at Valerio. He was no longer a haunting apparition on top of a pitcher's mound 60 feet 6 inches away. He was just a man. Valerio looked at Adam as if to ask, "You good?" Adam nodded and stepped back into the batter's box. His mind, free of oppressive fear, suddenly began to freely channel a lifetime of baseball instincts. His hands relaxed, and his lungs filled with an easy breath. Adam demanded the next pitch. He was locked and loaded.

After a lengthy at-bat, Adam finally got the pitch he wanted. He swung and shot the ball between the first and second basemen. He sprinted to first and sunk his cleats into the gleaming white base. His teammates roared. Sam fought back emotion. From the stands, he smiled and nodded. No one could possibly know just how big that was for Adam. Pride swelled within him as he watched his older brother, perched on first base, peeling off his batting gloves. As the fielders reorganized, Adam felt a wave of peace. He closed his eyes and savored it. *That was my first major league at-bat.* "It felt better than any other hit in my entire life," said Adam.

"It was scary, but I always take my lead from Adam," said Wendy about his facing De Los Santos for the second time. "I would talk to him before a game. If he wasn't nervous then I wasn't. It was a strange feeling, though, that game. Both of their lives were affected by that pitch. It had a huge impact on Valerio at the time too. Valerio thought he'd killed Adam. They both nodded to each other when Adam stepped into the batter's box. Then they went at it. Adam got a hit and got on base. They were two very classy players. They handled themselves as two true professionals. It was bittersweet."

As the season came to a close, Adam looked out over the Harbor Yard at the Bluefish stadium. He scanned the factory stacks spiking the skyline and leaned his head against his bag. He was spent. It had been six years since he'd been called up. He hit .259 for the Bluefish this season. He earned an on-base percentage of .390. He hit 15 triples and 10 home runs, but he was no longer the rising star who was ascending the ranks. He heard their whispers. He knew their talk. They were shrugging their shoulders and wondering when he was going to hang it up. *Hadn't he done enough?* Maybe it was over, and despite his extraordinary efforts, he was a one pitch guy after all. *Maybe it was time to face it and move on*, Adam told himself.

A maintenance worker who had no idea Adam was in

the stands hit the switch on the field lights. He was left in darkness. His bank account was dismal, but his company was growing. His wife was in a heated battle with the cancer that was trying to claim her twin sister's life. With the ball park lights out, Adam gazed up at the stars in the nighttime sky. They looked new and glimmered in a way he hadn't seen before. He stood up, shoveled his bag over his shoulder, and walked out of the ball park. He needed to speak with the mentor who could help him hear his own voice. He knew exactly who to call.

Adam reached out to his father on the way home and told him he was wrestling with the idea of walking away from the game. Mark's voice steadied and comforted him as it had done every day of his life. From his first steps and first falls to this moment, Adam's parents were always there to help him get up. This voice was what he needed to hear as he considered making one of the most significant choices of his life. Mark told him he had to do what he believed was right, and ultimately only Adam knew what that was. He said, "You've never taken time for yourself to heal. You don't have to call it quits, you can just give yourself time to get physically and mentally healthy. Just do what you need to do for you." Comforted, he knew he needed to speak with one more person before making a final decision.

With the little money he earned during the season, Adam bought a plane ticket to Sacramento, California, to see Dusty. They walked to a restaurant across the street from Dusty's home. The server poured two glasses of wine as they began talking baseball and Adam's setbacks in recent years. He ran his hand over the scar that wrapped his surgically repaired shoulder. While enduring an entire season playing with a torn rotator cuff, Adam described how the injury affected his swing and how he compensated for it, still producing significant numbers to contribute to the team. Dusty, like a wise father who loves his son enough to tell him the truth, set down his glass of wine and leaned in. "Even if you hit .330 in an independent league, you still might not get noticed, Adam. You're not going back to play independent ball. I know you can still play, but you're better than what you're getting from the game now. It's time to go start your life. Maybe down the road baseball will be there for you."

These were the words that stung with the truth Adam needed to hear. No one else could have communicated this to him. Dusty spent his entire life immersed in the business of baseball, and he'd never allowed it to rob him of his love for the game or his investment in the players he loved. Adam could not express how much Dusty's words meant to him or how his words affected him at this most pivotal time in his life. They reflected the truth Adam knew but hadn't been able to accept until now. "I can't specifically recall the details of that conversation because I was speaking from the heart. If it was only from the mind I would recall the details, but that was from the heart," Dusty said. He likened it to conversations he had with Hank Aaron. "Hank would often tell me, you may not understand what I'm telling you now, but retain the message. Someday you may understand later."

Adam thought back to the day the scout pointed to his chest and told his mother "It's what he's got in there that makes him different. His heart." He recalled playing on the Field of Dreams as a child and becoming consumed with a love for the game. Since the age of 13, Adam invested everything he had into baseball, and it had all been worth it. He met amazing people and played with the finest teammates. He reached the top of this mountain and gained a glimpse very few people ever earned the privilege of seeing. He was knocked off that mountain in the same split second. He fought and clawed to get back. In the process, he faced his most enormous fear by getting back into the batter's box against the same man who nearly killed him.

Adam discovered in that moment how the game gave him even a greater gift. It was a gift of partnership, teamwork, and inspiring others to reach the heights of their goals and dreams. His wife was his best friend, and his family's loyalty was unmatched. It was okay to walk away from his dream of playing Major League Baseball. It was time to let go. Adam stepped into the bronze California sunlight and watched the sun embed itself into the sea. The waves hushed all sound as Adam began to look within himself. He wondered what life had in store for him next.

In Adam's Own Words...

The person I have learned the most from is my father, Mark. I speak with him every day. His steady voice and presence stabilized me through every high and low of my journey. I am incredibly fortunate to have someone who answers the phone at any hour, calmly listens, and provides a voice of reason. He has done this throughout my life. Everyone needs an influence like this in their lives if they are going to persevere through adversity. He is not only my father, but he is a true friend. He was never a professional athlete but he played sports in high school and understands the mental side of the game. He understood the nuances and gave his opinion when I needed it. He cares about me too much to just tell me what I want to hear.

As the end of my baseball career drew near, my connection with Dusty was so valuable because of his ability to understand not just me, but the game and business of baseball. He took the time to understand what I was feeling, as well as my current environment, and advised me when it was time to start my life beyond the game. I will always be indebted to him for this connection, his friendship, and guidance.

- Adam

Team Israel

Free from the need to prepare for another season of baseball, Adam immersed himself in the development of Lurong Living. He'd found something which was just as engaging as the game he loved. By helping others achieve a higher quality of life, he became a potential teammate to each person he contacted.

One of those teammates was Dave Plumey, the owner of Shoreline Athletics, a cross-training facility in Branford, Connecticut. Adam stopped by his facility one day while searching for a place to continue to train and stay in shape. Dave didn't recognize the unassuming hometown hero in sweats and old running shoes standing in front of him. Yet they instantly clicked as they chatted about the type of training Shoreline offered.

After Adam made his way out of the facility, a member asked, "Do you know who that was?" Dave immediately rushed outside and flagged down Adam in the parking lot to invite him back inside. "I couldn't believe how humble he was. His work ethic is unparalleled," he marveled. He offered to train Adam one-on-one for free while introducing him to the world of CrossFit.

As their friendship developed, Adam learned Dave was dealing with inflammation and pain related to some calcium deposits which were discovered by a recent MRI. Adam suggested velvet deer antler. Skeptical at first, Dave was amazed at how effective it was for him. Dave and

Adam began to dream big about what their collective knowledge, history, and resources could accomplish. They began brainstorming the concept of a nationwide nutrition and fitness challenge.

In early 2012, Adam received a call on his cellphone from another potential teammate. He didn't recognize the number but picked up anyway. "Adam! Hey! My name is Matt Liston!" He began a high-energy barrage of admiration, rants against injustice, and repeated mentions of a social media campaign he wanted to create to get Adam an official major league at-bat.

Liston, a self-proclaimed baseball fanatic, wanted fans everywhere to sign a petition for Adam to get an official at-bat since he was robbed of the opportunity on his first attempt and was the only player in history to have his career end on the very first pitch. For Liston, no one who worked hard and long enough to make it to the majors should suffer the same fate that haunted "Moonlight" Graham. In 1905, he appeared as a right fielder in a single game in the major leagues but never got to step into the batter's box.

When Adam was hit in the head on the first pitch he faced, it was recorded as an official plate appearance but not an at-bat. While his on-base percentage was 1 for 1, a perfect 1.000, his batting average was a spotless 0 for 0. He never got a hit, and he never made an out. He never even got a chance to take a swing. Liston could not stomach the reality that the cruelty of life could end Adam's major league career with one pitch. Baseball was too sacred a game for that narrative to exist within its history, and he wanted to start a movement to help.

Adam wondered, *Who was this lunatic on the other end of the line, and who gave him my personal phone number?* As the conversation continued, Liston began to convince him that he wasn't entirely crazy. His motives were genuine and well-intentioned. Matt wanted to cement Adam's legacy as a professional player. Who knows where it would lead Adam's career from there? The idea was pretty far-fetched. It was a long shot on top of a long shot, but there was an uncomfortable appeal to it. These were the kind of odds Adam liked.

He'd always firmly believed that anything was possible. Countless times he'd told others about the importance of passion, how it can't be measured, and how it can make what is perceived to be impossible, achievable. Adam realized this idea unselfishly embodied everything he believed in. He knew he'd be a hypocrite if he dissuaded Liston from pursuing his dream of making this right. He also knew any amount of national attention could earn him a real opportunity to at least get back to a big league spring training camp to showcase his skills on the field.

Adam gave Liston his blessing to move forward, but the business of baseball just shook its head, initially dismissing the idea as spring training came and went. ESPN aired an *Outside the Lines* piece on July 9, 2012, commemorating the seventh anniversary of the 2005 at-bat during the All-Star break. Soon after it aired, Adam received a phone call from Liston. He was in the hospital at the time with Lindsay, Melissa and the Marottoli family for another procedure. Adam told him the piece was too depressing to watch, but Liston had other plans. "Check your email, I have something else for you," he said.

Liston forwarded a promotional video he'd created over the last few months called One at Bat. In a hospital waiting room, Adam was overcome with emotion as he saw people all over the country lobbying for him to get his second chance, despite missing spring training. He broke down at the sight of fans wearing t-shirts and putting up posters with his name on them. Even professional baseball players were offering up one of their own at-bats so Adam could have one. He was floored. They knew what he persevered through, and they knew he deserved this. Though he was consumed with Lurong Living and his first nationwide health challenge was taking shape, he called Liston back and told him he was officially all in.

Soon after, Adam received a phone call from Brad Ausmus, the current manager of the Detroit Tigers and former manager of the Israel national baseball team. Ausmus is a former professional catcher who spent 18 years in the major leagues. In 1999 he was voted into the All-Star game and earned a Gold Glove three times. Prior to playing professional baseball, he attended and graduated from Dartmouth College, earning a degree in Government. He is highly regarded as one of smartest men in all of baseball.

Ausmus had been hired to manage the Israeli team for the 2013 season. Ausmus learned of Adam's story and offered an invitation to try out for the upcoming World Baseball Classic. Excited by the opportunity, Adam became engaged by the idea of participating on the greatest Jewish baseball team at the time. He discussed the opportunity with Lindsay. Though it would mean some time away, combining the sport of baseball with Adam's Jewish heritage was too enticing to pass up. Lindsay sensed how much this opportunity meant to him. They agreed that regardless of any financial or family burden it created, it was well worth the investment.

Adam dug out a pair of cleats and laced them up. He drove to his old practice field, stretched, and began to train. Every morning he got up early, dismissing daily inconveniences and distractions. He silenced his sore muscles' discomfort with proper nutrition and velvet deer antler. The fire of Adam's will to play on Team Israel burned within him. He dedicated every sacrifice he made to those who had gone before him and who suffered so much to create all the blessings and opportunities he'd received. He wanted his own life to be an offering to those who would come after him. His commitment to the game of baseball was the gift he could give.

Adam knew in order to be able to give this gift, he needed to correct his swing. The time off and the adjustments he made to compensate for the lack of strength in his shoulder left his swing a mangled mess. Everything had gone haywire. His stance, swing, and approach all needed to be fixed. He knew the perfect person to help was the well-known hitting coach Wally Horsman.

Adam valued Wally because he knew how to diagnose both the swing and the player. Every professional gets out of sync at times, especially after an injury or extended time off. Players often make it more physically difficult for themselves by getting buried inside their own head. Wally knew Adam as both a player and a person and in ten minutes, he was able to dissect the flawed swing mechanics. During the next three days, he returned Adam to his old form. His confidence soared. He felt like he was the player he was in 2005.

While his team at Lurong Living was busy launching its first nationwide challenge, Adam felt ready to take on the world and reported to West Palm Beach for try-outs to earn a slot on the Israeli team's roster. Ausmus recognized right away that Adam possessed "tremendous energy." He was "positive and smiling at all times." It was clear to Ausmus his "love of baseball hadn't waned."

Upon arrival, Adam began to learn how the team was unifying people in a region where there was so much hatred. He learned how sportsmanship was being used as a mechanism to alleviate differences and bring people together. His Jewish heritage had always served as inspiration for him to get up when he was down, especially as he studied a culture that suffered so many greater challenges than those he faced in his own life. He excelled offensively, spraying hits all over the field, and wreaking havoc on the basepaths. His defense in the outfield was spectacular. He earned a spot on Team Israel's roster.

Adam played an important role on Team Israel because he was one of the more veteran guys on the team. "He provided valuable leadership to the younger players because of his experience," according to Ausmus. The team united and began to prepare for a run at the qualifying tournament for the 2013 World Baseball Classic.

As he played, Adam recollected his days at the University of North Carolina. He thought about the first time he'd encountered religion blended with athletics and how his Jewish heritage differed from other faiths and cultures gathering on the baseball field. Adam treasured the time with fellow Jewish teammates playing the game he loved. He swelled with pride, motivated and empowered by their shared history, and determined to help his team get through the qualifying rounds and into the World Baseball Classic. For Adam, it was an honor that went beyond words.

He continued to be amazed at the overwhelming response to Lurong Living from people across the country, eager to join together to succeed in achieving their health and fitness goals. All the lessons he'd learned during his baseball career had armed him with the tools to create a movement helping thousands of people reach their highest potential. Meanwhile, Liston pressed on with his One at Bat campaign. More than 27,000 people had signed the petition and the front office of the Miami Marlins became intrigued.

Adam's phone rang. It was 11:30 p.m. on a Sunday night. Liston was calling to ask when he was going to be out of the locker room. Slightly irritated, Adam said he'd be out soon. Adam looked around the locker room at the guys who just lost a chance to play in the World Baseball Classic. They'd been narrowly eliminated from the qualifying tournament by Spain in extra innings, and the wound was still fresh in their hearts and minds. Not only that, but this was most likely Adam's last game in organized baseball. He needed to be with his teammates a little while longer as they regrouped emotionally and said their goodbyes.

In Adam's Own Words...

We must not allow ourselves to be scared of others. We must find our similarities and value our differences. To allow hate to exist is to severely limit our ability to personally and collectively grow and change. When we take time to share our journeys we find common ground and enlightenment, like in my experience playing with Team Israel. I will always feel a deep sense of pride and honor to have been a part that team. To participate with other Jewish men playing the game of baseball was to be part of the process of suppressing hate through athletics.

When people share their journeys, the world becomes less intimidating. We are less isolated. We learn how others overcame challenges similar to those we are facing. We become inspired by human bravery and motivated by a vision of what is possible. Our problems are less scary when we realize how common they are. Achievements we once thought were impossible become less challenging than we thought. Positive connections with people empower us to fulfill our goals and reach the potential within us. Although others may have their opinions, at the end of the day it is only ourselves contending with whom we have been, what we've done, and what we still have left to do.

– Adam

One at Bat!

When Adam came out of the locker room, Liston was grinning ear to ear. He asked if Adam would go on camera for a short exit interview about his experience with Team Israel. He agreed, but made it clear that he wasn't in the best mood as the loss was still on his mind. They were finishing the brief video when Liston's phone lit up. Adam glanced at the name. It was David Samson, the president of the Miami Marlins since 2002. "Adam's story always intrigued me," said Samson. Knowing Adam's injury was sustained while playing against the team then known as the Florida Marlins, he knew his club was also a part of the story.

Adam's heart began to race. Liston's grin only got bigger. Adam felt the same silly grin start to make its way onto his own face. Liston answered the phone and put it on speaker so they both could hear. After learning of the One at Bat campaign, team owner Jeffrey Loria, Samson, and their staff decided to give Adam his shot. Loria and Samson loved the game of baseball, and they loved those who loved it back. What mattered to them was the joy of the game. What mattered was a ball, a bat and an opportunity. Adam would get his. They would proudly give the five foot eight and three quarter inch tall Jewish kid the opportunity to claim what he earned. The young man from Guilford, Connecticut, who loved the game with everything he ever was, deserved it.

Adam wasn't going to be left without an at-bat like "Moonlight" Graham. It was more important to Samson, on a personal level, to give Adam the opportunity because "We in the Marlins organization constantly think about how hard these athletes work. We know how hard it is to reach the major leagues. We also know how hard it is to *stay* there. Adam is a young man who worked very hard to get there, and he never got an opportunity to have a complete at-bat."

Samson told Adam he was present during his debut with the Cubs. They followed his career as he battled to get back. Their scouts kept tabs on him as he rehabbed, struggled, and healed. They watched him continue for years to take batting practice like it was the World Series, hustle for every fly ball, and run hard with every opportunity he got. Adam had no idea and recalled the J.C. Watts quote: "Do what's right, especially when no one's looking." He was glad he'd held himself to that standard. He hadn't known it, but someone had been watching the entire time.

Samson asked Adam if he would honor the Miami Marlins by joining their team on October 2, 2012 for a one-day contract to be announced live in several days to a nationwide television audience. Reeling, Adam stammered his thanks. He stared at Liston. Was this real?

Adam and Lindsay often experienced exciting, positive news while simultaneously grappling with tragedy. Later that night they were notified that recent scan results showed Melissa had developed a new series of tumors. The cancer continued to metastasize from her lungs to her brain. She already survived one surgery shortly after her initial diagnosis, and her family was confronted with the brutal reality of what another one might mean for her. As he traveled home and prepared for the upcoming announcement, they did their best to cope with conflicting feelings of joy and agony.

On the morning of September 27, 2012, Adam and Liston found themselves being welcomed into NBC's *Today* studio in New York City by Matt Lauer. It was very real. Lauer is a prominent television journalist who currently hosts *Today* and contributes to NBC's television program Dateline. When Adam was hit during his first major league plate appearance, Lauer and a friend who worked on *Today* kept the story in their minds. Lauer later fondly remembered how his story "came back to me." As viewers tuned into *Today* that morning, they didn't know a story was about to inspire them. They didn't know they were about to experience one of the most unique stories in the history of professional sports. They would experience a moment where they revisited some of their earliest childhood and family memories of a game called baseball.

Today viewers would not only revisit those memories, but they would identify with Adam's relentless pursuit of the American dream even after his winning moments were infiltrated by life's traumas and challenges. Every person who has worked tirelessly to achieve a dream could identify with Adam and the struggles he had to overcome to be in that moment. They understood that his appearance on *Today* was an opportunity for a horrible wrong to be made right. This was a moment of respect, value, and humanity. It represented the reasons why people love the game of baseball. He hadn't merely earned another opportunity for a major league at-bat, he'd earned the respect of those who knew the value and significance of it.

"People need to understand something about the Marlins' decision. Adam had been working to get back for *seven years*. This wasn't some gimmick. He was a major leaguer. We at the Marlins value hard work and perseverance. We believe that anything is possible," said Samson. Liston's campaign had struck a chord with sports fans everywhere, whether they were originally familiar with Adam's story or not. People loved the idea of creating an opportunity for Adam Greenberg, a former Major League Baseball player, to finally get his official at-bat. As the story grew, Matt Lauer noticed.

As Adam took his place on the *Today* show stage, Lauer didn't know what to expect. He wondered if Adam would say he deserved the at-bat or justify it based on the struggles he'd been through. That wasn't the case at all. Lauer soon learned Adam loved the game of baseball far too much to tarnish the moment with even a shred of self-pity. Lauer challenged Adam with the questions skeptical baseball fans would ask when they learned of the campaign. He countered every challenge with the humble and noble spirit behind the movement. This was not a publicity stunt. It was a moment where skepticism could only serve to uncover the unflinching truth that this was one of the purest demonstrations of the love of the game in all of its storied history.

Live on air, Lauer introduced David Samson, who offered Adam an at-bat with the Marlins on October 2, 2012. "And believe me, you're gonna get one at-bat, so get ready," he advised. Samson and Loria, felt it was only right for Adam to have this opportunity in a Miami uniform. Adam's reaction surpassed all expectations. He thanked Samson and Loria for the opportunity, assured Samson he would be ready, and reaffirmed how Major League Baseball "didn't owe me anything." Adam said, "From the bottom of my heart, I can't express how much it means to me."

Although others may have seen the moment as a prime business opportunity to reach millions of people with a product, Adam refused to let the moment be about anything other than the game of baseball and his desire to continue to play it. Even with just a measly 100 dollars in his bank account, Adam refused to desecrate this sacred offering no matter how badly he was suffering financially. This was for the love of the game. It was too pure, just as Jeffrey Loria, David Samson, and Peter Gammons recognized it to be. "We weren't looking for a mockery," Samson said. "We were looking for a moment."

That was the moment Lauer recognized the depth of character of the young man sitting in front of him. "That really struck me," he said. "This young man persevered through some incredibly unfortunate circumstances, battled back without bitterness, and kept plugging away. He recovered, went back to work, and learned valuable lessons from the adversity he faced along the way."

"I felt good all over," Lauer said. "People reacted to this. There was a huge response to the segment. People were calling, emailing us, sending us notes. They were all saying the same thing. They were unanimously praising Adam and the Marlins. People went to work that day feeling great about the world after seeing that. It contained all the elements of a perfect *Today* show segment. A wonderful human being had been given a second chance. It was one of the most memorable segments of my career." When Gammons heard what Loria and Samson had done, he was overjoyed. "Thanks to the Marlins for giving Adam Greenberg his richly-deserved at-bat. It will be an intensely human moment. Thanks Jeffrey Loria," Gammons tweeted.

"Most of us can't conceive the results of concussions," Gammons said. He recalled speaking with other players who experienced similar trauma. He said other players described dropping routine fly balls, attempting to cope with the fear of the batter's box afterward, and battling persistent symptoms. "Adam had astounding courage to get back in the batter's box after his career was robbed from him. That type of bravery should not be taken for granted."

Before he knew it, Adam was in back-to-back interviews with various media outlets all over New York City. At every turn, Liston's camera crew was there filming his every move. Adam forced himself to compartmentalize his emotions as the world embraced him, attempting to fully experience and reciprocate the joy of the moment.

Everyone involved loved the game far too much to reduce it to anything less than what it was. It was a brilliant moment for baseball. It was an opportunity where truly anything could happen. Few sensed it as powerfully as Adam's own family. The trauma of his first major league plate appearance extended beyond the boundary of Adam's body. The blast concussed everyone who loved him. For the second time in their lives they found themselves packing, planning and organizing travel to Florida to watch him play Major League Baseball.

In Adam's Own Words...

We can persevere through adversity by deriving strength from the positive influences in our lives. We can refuse to be dominated by pain, confusion, animosity, and fear. Together, we can acknowledge our emotions while preventing ourselves from becoming enslaved by them. Life will go on with or without us, so why not make the best of it? Why waste the precious time we have with defeat?

Every moment is both a gift and an opportunity. Things we never thought were possible are at our fingertips. Don't tell your dream how to arrive, just know it will be realized. It may arrive in a shape or form you didn't foresee. It may even surprise you by being better than what you expected.

– Adam

Dream On

Loren scrambled to buy plane tickets. Tucked into the excitement and joy was a shred of anxiety. She recalled how the Cubs gave the Greenbergs the celebratory treatment the evening prior to Adam's first plate appearance. She pictured the family room and the seats next to other players' wives and family. She remembered the epic excitement of the moment and getting chills as she watched her brother appear in the on-deck circle before making his way to the batter's box.

Loren thought back to being on the phone with Keri. She paused from packing as she recalled the terrifying moment when Adam was hit. She watched frantically as her brother lay on the ground clutching his head. She would never be able to forget experiencing that height of euphoria eclipsed by sheer terror. She marveled that these two very different emotions could be welded together inside the same second. She recalled watching Adam struggle with something as simple as tying his shoes while at home during the All-Star break. "He never talked about it, and it was really hard to see him like that," she said. This time would be different. It would not happen again, she told herself.

Adam's family and friends were soon assembling in Florida where the Marlins staff, coaches, and players welcomed them to Marlins Park. Adam was moved with emotion as he saw Lindsay's father, Sal, who came all the way from Connecticut to support his son-in-law. He was in the middle of one of the most trying times of his entire life, fighting to keep his daughter alive as she fought cancer, and still selflessly made the journey.

Although Sal referred to himself as "not the most sophisticated of baseball fans," he was amazed at the Marlins' kindness and impressed by the processes associated with preparing for a major league game. "The night before, they gave us the entire stadium and told us, 'Just lock up when you leave,'" he marveled. Adam, Sam, and Sal walked onto the field together. They had the brand new stadium all to themselves. "We were like three kids playing sandlot baseball," he said. "It was extraordinary."

As they played catch, Sal thought about how much he'd looked forward to this trip. Adam had done so much to support his family during their battle against cancer. Sal was appreciative of the small opportunity to give something back. As he watched Adam and Sam on the field, he thought about how he was doing everything he could as a father to get Melissa the best treatment available and guide his family through their difficult time. When the pain was at its worst, Sal often made a point of reminding his family there would also be days that were better and lighthearted. There would be days like this when good things happened they could enjoy together. They needed to make the most of these moments to sustain themselves through the trying times.

After returning to their hotel, Adam began mentally

preparing for the next day's game. He was still concerned the Marlins players may not accept him and view him as a distraction or a gimmick. Adam wasn't concerned about the media's opinion. What meant the most to him were his peers. What would they truly think about all this?

As Adam entered the ballpark the next day, he was greeted by relief pitcher Heath Bell. Heath was one of the highest paid players on the team. He told Adam he'd come to the stadium early just to meet him. As he made heartfelt introductions to every player and coach they encountered, Heath made it clear to Adam that he wasn't just meeting Marlins players. He was meeting Adam's *teammates*. One day contract or not, it didn't matter. Adam was a major leaguer, and today this was *his* team. He was moved beyond words and humbled by Heath's exceptional kindness.

Before heading out onto the field, Adam and Sam found the cages underneath the stadium for some early indoor swings. Sam helped him warm up with some knuckleballs in preparation to face R.A. Dickey. Afterward Sam remembered watching his older brother walk from the dugout into the light of field to join his team for on-field batting practice. "Hey Greenberg, you can't leave the cage until you hit one out!" Marlins catcher John Buck shouted during Adam's turn at the plate. John and Adam had been teammates during his time with the Kansas City Royals. Adam grinned, locked in, and waited for the next pitch. He unleashed his powerful swing and sent the ball on a flight path that landed well beyond the right field wall. "That didn't take long," they laughed as they all headed back into the locker room.

The clubhouse buzzed with individual conversations as the team got dressed and prepared for the game at their lockers. John Buck was determined to make sure there was no question in anyone's mind that his teammate deserved to wear a major league uniform. John stood up and began addressing the team on his own. He described in detail how he'd played with Adam in the Royals organization. "Adam was a professional and earned the right to be here," he told them. John stressed to the other players that Adam was their teammate, and that was how it was going to be.

Moved by John's speech, Heath stood up and spoke next on Adam's behalf. "Adam was a player, and this was no charity," he said. This was no gimmick to sell more tickets. This was about the very core of what was special and spectacular about the game of baseball. Heath then offered Adam fair warning that a customary hazing ritual which "may or may not" involve a Speedo, swimming goggles, and the song "Gangnam Style" was about to begin. Adam groaned. "I have no rhythm. This is gonna be brutal," he laughed.

Another teammate stood up. Then another. Adam felt like he was in a movie. He fought back his emotions as one by one a room full of his peers honored seven agonizing years of struggle. John ordered Adam to climb up on the table in front of them, and the music began to blare from the clubhouse speakers. He performed a rhythmless, seemingly endless dance while his new teammates laughed and cheered their approval. Adam had officially earned the right to wear a Marlin jersey. When all the laughing subsided, the team finished getting ready.

Adam sat down in front of his locker and took a quiet moment to himself. He marveled at his journey. In 2005, he hadn't had time to be hazed by his new team. This one, who he'd only met a few hours ago, had fully embraced him. His biggest worry dissolved. Game time approached and his family took their seats in the stands. Wendy was moved with emotion when Coach Fox appeared in the stands to greet the family he'd stayed in touch with throughout Adam's journey. Coach Fox made the trip from North Carolina and considered it one the most memorable events in his entire career.

"Adam, to this day, continues to impact the Tar Heels organization," he said. "Adam's is a great story of perseverance. Our players and our prospective players know his story because I make a point of telling each of them. Life can be cruel. Life can be unfair. All we are promised is today. You can do all the right things, and your dream may or may not come true. I respect Adam because he hasn't allowed himself to become bitter. He uses what has happened to him to help others. He worked his hardest and his career in baseball ended much too soon, but that's life. The same characteristics he possessed and practiced that got him to the big leagues are now helping him have an immense impact in people's lives beyond baseball. He has an unbelievable ability to take the difficult and unique things which have happened to him and transform them into something which helps others."

"I think I've never seen this ballclub more excited than today," Ozzie Guillen, the Marlins manager, told a reporter from the Washington Post. This was about honoring a Major League Baseball player who had given everything he had to the game. This was an embrace and a thank you to Adam by people at every level who shared a love of the game. This was the game of baseball telling Adam everything he endured wasn't all for nothing. "Adam was a big leaguer. He earned and deserved every right to be in the major leagues. So for me, Adam's One at Bat at Marlin's Park was priceless," said Keith Miller. "I think his story needs to get out there. I'm glad it's being told."

Adam stood for every person hustling and striving to achieve their goals and their dreams. Everyone knew what it was like to have something they loved dearly taken from them. They knew how hard it was to achieve a dream and how cruel life could be. It didn't matter if Adam launched a homerun out of the park, hit a bloop single, or struck out. Stepping into the batter's box for this at-bat was about hope, yielding an unparalleled power to connect, liberate, and inspire.

The media asked Dickey, the dominant knuckleball pitcher from the New York Mets, how he would pitch Adam. Without hesitation, he responded "I'll pitch him like the big leaguer that he is." These were *professional* baseball players. Years prior, while Adam reeled from the effects of traumatic brain injury, he was accused by some of not being worthy of these professional ranks. Adam took comfort in the fact that those who played this game at the highest level had a very different opinion. They knew he was one of them.

As Sam watched his brother approach the on-deck circle, he remembered having the honor of playing on the same team with Adam on in Bridgeport. Sam remembered Adam always wanting to go "ten steps past what people thought could happen." He remembered hearing Adam say, "You are what you believe. That comes from inside of you. At the end of the day you need a goal. If you believe enough, your goal will take you where you want to be. Don't just go through the motions. Get up. Get after it."

Adam's goals and laser focused determination brought him *here*. Relentless positivity bent conventional laws of ascent to the major leagues, and here he was in a Marlins uniform. Aerosmith's "Dream On" thundered throughout the stadium as Max thought about how different this at-bat was as compared to the first. When they got the news Adam was getting called up for the first time, he drove through the night in the pouring rain to link up with his family. There was no nervousness. This was what he worked his entire life to earn. This is what made sense. Adam deserved it, and he was going to get it.

The second time around was different. Max was nervous. He didn't want the public to see this as a gimmick. His brother worked too hard and too long to be treated like that. After watching the media pieces and speaking with Matt Liston, he was relieved to see no one was treating Adam's life that way. To see professional baseball players saying into the camera that Adam *deserved* an at-bat and that they would willingly give up one of theirs for him proved he wasn't being treated as some kind of pity case but as a fellow player.

Max also thought about how special it was that this was not just Adam earning his way back on his own. It was also about others who knew everything he had been through, supporting him to receive something they felt he deserved and earned. He thought about how Jeffrey Loria, David Samson, Matt Liston, and others who were offering their hand to Adam in order to heave him up and off the ground, just as Adam had done for him on the Guilford basketball court. Adam had never stopped sprinting, swinging, and sweating for *seven years*. Max and Sam looked at each other in disbelief as the crowd started screaming Adam's name and chanting "One at Bat! One at Bat!" "It was surreal," Max said, flooded with emotion. He couldn't help but smile as he thought about how every day his brother woke up and chose to stay positive, no matter what he faced. Adam knew if he believed it, he could make it happen. Here it was, happening.

Keri watched her younger brother get loose in the on-deck circle. She teared up as she pointed Adam out to her young son. She remembered Adam's relentless work ethic through high school, college, and the minor leagues.

She remembered being sickened by the endless sports newsreel at the restaurant she went to after her exam. She remembered his quiet defiance of anyone telling him he wasn't good enough or he wouldn't make it. Here he was, about to face R.A. Dickey. Keri knew this was more than just a baseball story. This was a story about conquering fear, pain, injury, and doubt. No matter what happened, it was a win. Adam wasn't just there to prove he could make it back, his simple presence was concrete proof that *anything* is possible.

Loren surveyed an entire stadium standing on their feet in anticipation. She wiped tears away and looked at her father who was doing the same. His son was ready to confidently carve his cleats into a major league batter's box once again. He remembered his young teenager in the backyard and basement, swinging his bat chanting *bat speed, bat speed, bat speed.* He was now a man, and tens of thousands of people were screaming at the top of their lungs, praying he would hit a baseball into the farthest reaches of Marlin's Park.

Wendy savored every step on the field. She knew how much Adam appreciated every mile she put on her minivan, shuttling him from tournament to game to practice. It was all worth it. It seemed like only yesterday he was nine years old in the back of the family car on the way to a karate tournament. While they tried to prepare him for the sting of life's inevitable losses, with gratitude, he showed them how he could win.

Lindsay's eyes sailed the sea of people in Marlins Park. One at Bat posters peppered the stands. Not only was a stadium of strangers demonstrating their support for Adam, but it had been the city of Miami, the entire Marlins organization, professional players who'd been in the league for years, and so many fans across the country. She marveled at the amount of respect everyone was showing her husband and his family.

When Lindsay watched Adam walk into the stadium earlier that day to take batting practice, she couldn't help feeling a twinge of sadness. This was what he wanted his whole life. He dreamed of going to the ball park, taking batting practice, preparing for, and playing the game he loved with everything he had. He'd invested his entire self into it, and it had been taken from him on his first major league pitch. As Adam blasted a homerun into the stands during batting practice, her sadness evaporated. His beaming smile was too bright. It was like he told her so many times as they faced pain, confusion, and frustration, "It didn't profit anyone to become bitter. What counted was to overcome."

In this moment, she craved Melissa's presence as visions of childhood Yankees games with her sister flashed into her mind. Melissa was too sick to attend the game in person, but she gathered with friends, family and local news reporters at the Guilford Mooring restaurant to celebrate Adam's day and watch the game. It comforted her to know she was there in spirit and watching the game surrounded by family. The announcer's booming voice called Adam's name over the chorus of Steven Tyler's epic ballad. Chills ran up her arms as Lindsay watched her husband dig into the batter's box. She wiped away the tears. He'd done it. He made it back to the major leagues. She closed her eyes for a brief second to fully appreciate the moment.

Matt Lauer recalled watching Adam step into the batter's box. "I had goosebumps. I remember thinking that anything can happen here, and even if he doesn't get a hit, it's still great. It was a wonderful moment of achievement. Adam is a role model. He's polite, respectful, has character. He's the type of guy you want your kids to hang out with. I was so proud of him. No matter what happened in that moment, everybody won."

"R.A. Dickey on the mound. Adam Greenberg in the box. Here we go.

First pitch. Strike one.

You knew he had to take a pitch. Words can't describe that last moment.

All the adrenaline.

All the excitement that's gotta be going through Adam Greenberg right now.

Dickey 0-1 pitch. And Greenberg takes a swing and a miss.

He's behind in the count 0-2.

0-2 pitch. Swing and a miss. And he strikes out.

But you know what? He made it back, he got his one at-bat.

And the crowd comes to their feet again."

Adam walked back to dugout, beaming. "It seemed he was able to get some closure," said Lauer. "Adam had his moment. He got his at-bat. I just wish it wasn't against the Cy Young winner that year."

"He had his hacks and R.A Dickey pitched him like a big leaguer.

He may be the only big leaguer in history with a smile that wide after striking out."

Adam was congratulated in the dugout by some of the most epic names in baseball. He knew he would never have to wrestle with what could've been. He felt light, free.

"He got that dancing knuckleball that stayed up in the zone, and it just took off.

But he had two good hacks on those last two knuckleballs. Good for him."

"Adam represents the perfect example of what this game is all about," said David Bell. "When team members strive to do their individual best to contribute to their team's success, they will become part of a team that is not only inspirational to each other but to the fans. This game can make a difference in our communities and the nation.

What people need to understand about Adam's individual career in baseball is that he was a *complete* success. Success looks different for each person. To walk away with no regrets and to know you gave everything you had—that's a great feeling. It doesn't matter whether you walk away a Hall of Famer or not."

In Adam's Own Words...

We should always trust in the reasons behind the dreams we set out to realize. Our dreams can be empowering if we involve the right people. Start with those around us who carry the most significance and meaning in our lives. Be sure to seek out dreams that can help invest time and energy into others. If our dreams don't benefit others in some way, then we're selfishly isolating and alienating ourselves.

Intentionally investing in another person must not be an attempt to convince ourselves how awesome we are. It must truly be something which edifies both involved. I strive to impart knowledge and change to others who will gain something good from it. As we all work together to achieve our dreams in life, recognize that the achievement may not occur right away. Don't give up! Be patient and comfortable with the process. Your dreams will be realized when the timing is right.

– Adam

Never Give Up

The crowd continued to shower Adam with applause as he tipped his Marlins cap from the top stair of the dugout.

"At 31, he would like to make a comeback. He did not play this year.

He had shoulder surgery after playing in the independent leagues.

He started a business but he started to train midway through the season.

Played with Israel in the World Baseball Classic team."

"Hey, don't worry about it. Congratulations, you did it!" Guillen said, while nodding at R.A. Dickey, who would go on to win 20 games and the National League Cy Young Award that year. "He's done the same thing to over 200 other guys already." Adam couldn't contain his smile. He finally got his official at-bat. He worked his entire life for it.

"There was someone who was very instrumental, in kind of his comeback.

And establishing himself, just as a citizen, and a business man. Dusty Baker.

Dusty Baker was his manager with the Cubs the night he was hit on July 9, 2005.

And Baker kept in contact and kept pushing him whenever the phone would ring.

Whenever he thought Greenberg needed a lift. Baker would reach out.

It was Dusty Baker that actually told Greenberg 'Look, you have a family now.

You might want to start your business and then think about coming back.'

And that's what he's done.

You mention his parents are here, his wife, other family members, many, many friends."

"Yes, Adam didn't hit a homerun, but it didn't matter," Lindsay recalled. What mattered was the police officer on the streets of New York City who saw the *Today* interview and told Adam afterwards "Nice job. We're rooting for you." It was the flight attendant on the plane to Florida who handed them a complimentary bottle of wine and thanked Adam for inspiring her ten-year-old son. She watched *Today* every day, and her son never watched with her, she said. The morning he was on the show was the first time her son watched a whole segment. She said her son couldn't stop smiling afterwards. Inspired, the child told his mother that if Adam could do what he had done, then he felt like he could accomplish anything too.

What mattered were the 27,118 people who signed a petition to get Adam his One at Bat and their willingness to put up signs and flyers all over their cities in support of him. What mattered was Adam's cleats finally taking their rightful place in a major league batter's box after a tenacious seven-year battle to overcome a head injury resulting in debilitating headaches, involuntary eye movements, positional vertigo, and uncontrollable physical symptoms. What mattered was making the most of every moment, none of it guaranteed, and having gratitude for the gift of his journey.

Adam's family wiped the tears out of their eyes. They knew why Adam got the fan mail he did, especially from young people. He also was small once, facing a giant world. Unintimidated, he faced all of it with respect and began to carve out his own place. He symbolized that even if you're smaller or lesser in whatever way, with dedication and perseverance, the circumstance you thought was your weakness instead can become your greatest strength. It was as if he enjoyed being underestimated because he knew that gave him an advantage. It was like he was saying, "Go ahead and underestimate me, after we battle you will not."

"And it's fun to watch the Marlins players embrace Greenberg.

The Marlin players, to their credit, accepted him into the clubhouse.

Hazed him a little bit, I think they made him sing a karaoke song.

Just a little rookie hazing.

And they had a great time with him during batting practice.

They all fell apart when on his last batting practice swing, he hit one out of the park."

Lauer pointed out why he thinks Adam's story resonates with so many. "Adam represents what we all *can* be. He is grateful for every opportunity. He uses his hard knocks to channel himself into being a better person. Goodness wins out. Perseverance should not be forgotten." As the television cameras followed him toward the post-game media interviews, Adam knew what was possible. *Anything.* "It was magical. The energy that was in the stadium is something that I've never experienced in my life. Everyone that was there, I think, probably felt the same thing. You could just feel the genuine support. It was awesome," Adam told a room full of reporters before calling into ESPN for a live on-air interview on SportsCenter.

"I'm not even sure you're aware of this, Adam, but maybe this is one of the coolest things to happen to you today. Topps baseball card company has come out and said they're going to include you in this season's series, and you will have a big league baseball card with the Marlins. How's that feel?" SportsCenter asked. Childhood memories of collecting, studying, and sorting the cards of his favorite players flooded into Adam's mind. He could barely contain his emotions. "Oh man, we all dream about that when we're growing up, and I never did get one when I was a big leaguer with the Cubs so that's really an amazing gesture by

Topps. I'm honored, humbled, privileged, all of the above, to have them include me in this season."

As the final flock of cameramen and reporters wandered away, Adam joined family and friends at the scheduled after-party at The Clevelander which sat just beyond the left field fence. As those closest to him honored the day's achievement, Adam knew he would cherish this day and night forever. Afterward, Adam made his way back to his hotel room where his family and friends continued to celebrate privately. Wendy retrieved something she'd been saving for a long time. It was the bottle of Dom Perignon champagne they never had the chance to open in 2005. Surrounded by his loved ones, they cracked the bottle open, and raised their glasses high.

Adam was exhausted, but he couldn't stop smiling. Adam earned the honor of playing on Team Israel in West Palm Beach, and some of the finest men in Major League Baseball gave him an opportunity to have an official at-bat in Miami. He thought of all the people he'd met that day and all the friends and family who helped him enjoy one of the most unique moments in all of Major League Baseball history. Unable to sleep, Adam marveled at reality.

Dusty had been right. "Maybe baseball will be there for you down the line," he told Adam after the 2011 season. Who knew the bronze sun that set that day in California would rise brilliantly again in Florida? "Now that's fighting your way back," Baker said. "I've seen a lot quit along the way. He's a different young man than most. That shows his love for the game to play and compete. He will take that same love and joy into his marriage and fatherhood. He'll instill it in his son."

The love of the game that was handed down from Ausmus' grandfather to his mother to him led to a unique understanding of the significance of even one major league at-bat. "When Adam got his second chance, it was a testament to his ability to persevere. I was pulling for him. I was hoping he'd hit a homerun." In thinking about all he endured as he pursued a career in baseball, Ausmus credited Adam for not giving up. "Adam could've easily given up on his dream, but he didn't. He should be proud that even though his career was cut short he continued to battle against the odds. Playing with Team Israel was a part of that. People should know that persistence pays off. No one should give up on their dream."

"Although he may not have been able at that time to fill a permanent spot on a roster, this was a former major leaguer who deserved a *moment*. We wanted to create a moment where anything was possible. We wanted to give that to Adam and our fans," said Samson. On October 2, 2012, they succeeded. "Adam was able to close the loop. His dream came true. As people think about his life, I would like them to know first just how hard it is to be a successful hitter at the major league level. Second, I would like them to use Adam's example as a conduit for their own life. Once they discover what they can do and what they should do, they can put in the work to achieve it. Don't give up," Samson continued.

Adam donated his day of professional baseball salary to the Marlins Foundation and the Sports Legacy Institute which works to study, treat, and prevent the effects of brain trauma in athletes. It didn't surprise Samson. "Adam's financial donation, although significant and consistent with his character, was only a small portion of what he invested in the game of baseball. His legacy is one of perseverance. He truly has no detractors. His life is a great lesson for children and people around the world. He never just talked about doing it. He just did it. He went after his dream," Samson said.

As Adam closed his eyes to seal every image, sound, and smell of the day into his memory, he heard Lindsay hang up the phone. In the quiet of the night, she began softly crying. Adam would finish celebrating his triumph later. It was time to comfort his wife. Melissa's cancer symptoms had worsened. Adam and Lindsay returned to Connecticut to help the Marottoli family care for her.

Within two weeks of arriving home, Melissa returned to the hospital where the family remained by her side for the next 55 days. They lived at the hospital and made the most of every moment. She died December 9, 2012, surrounded by the love of her family and friends. A majority of people who are diagnosed with Stage IV lung cancer succumb to the disease within one year. Melissa lived *five*.

Lindsay, Adam, and the Marottoli family created the Melissa Marottoli Hogan Foundation in her honor. The foundation tirelessly supports advancements in immunotherapy and education. They continually transform the pain of losing Melissa into comfort, hope, and strength for families fighting for their very own. "She was stronger than anyone, including herself, expected her to be," Lindsay said of Melissa. "A cure would've been the home run, yes. Sometimes life doesn't give you the home run. Sometimes the victory is simply knowing that you gave everything you had, and there are no regrets. What matters is that you left everything you had on the field, in the hospital, with friends and loved ones who are giving everything they have right back to you. Sometimes the home run is simply refusing to give up," Adam said.

In Adam's Own Words...

For most of my early years, I *had to have* Major League Baseball. But who knows what you and I will *have to have* tomorrow? I love the fact that my experiences have afforded me the endless opportunity to connect with others who are facing adversity, allowing me to use experiences like these to change lives through the power of positivity, perseverance, and nutrition.

Whether trying to achieve a specific health goal or overcome a hurdle in life, sports, or business, I enjoy being able to help others while expecting nothing in return. It is truly a privilege to have met so many amazing people, fueling my desire to keep making real contributions to the health, joy, and satisfaction of every single person I get the opportunity to interact with.

– Adam

A Greater Calling

Confident he had what it took to continue at the highest level after playing for Team Israel and the Miami Marlins, Adam headed to the 2012 Baseball Winter Meetings in Nashville, Tennessee. He secured Alex Gonzalez as his agent and networked his way into a meeting with Brady Anderson and Buck Showalter of the Baltimore Orioles. They were looking for a speedy, late-inning outfielder with strong defensive skills. Armed with statistics, Gonzalez told them Adam was the perfect fit.

He returned to Connecticut hopeful about his chances to get an invite to spring training. Just days later, Melissa passed away peacefully. As they grieved her loss and honored her life at her funeral, Adam's cell phone vibrated with a text message from his agent asking if he could "really play" defense. His phone vibrated again with an incoming call. Adam knew Alex wouldn't be calling unless it was important. Later that night his agent apologized for bothering him at such a sacred time, but he wanted to tell Adam the good news. "You're a Baltimore Oriole." He'd been offered an invitation to minor league spring training in Sarasota, Florida, the following season. He marveled at how many times in his life he received the greatest of news during the most difficult of times.

Adam found success in camp, averaging .355 at the plate and earning an on-base percentage of .413. He never paid much attention to or even kept track of spring training stats, but this time was different. Knowing the odds were stacked against him, this was about proving to himself he could play at the major league level, regardless of what anyone else thought. With each hit, catch, and sprint, Adam continued to quietly prove in his heart of hearts he was a major leaguer.

Adam was surrounded by more than a dozen other major league outfielders, all playing at a high level, and all seeking their own dreams. As camp came to a close, five or six went on to make the major league roster. Four or five more each made Triple-A, then Double-A. Too many big leaguers accepted their offered assignments to make room for Adam, and he was too old for Double-A. It was a numbers game, and he was on the outside looking in.

Once again, Adam was offered a job to coach rather than play. It was time to walk away. He proved to himself he had what it took, but his career of playing Major League Baseball was over. It would consist of one pitch with the Chicago Cubs and one at-bat with the Miami Marlins. So be it. He was satisfied. He knew he could lay his head down at night confident in his abilities and the decision to hang up his cleats. Adam Greenberg officially retired from professional baseball.

Adam walked up the stairs and strode toward the center of the stage. He adjusted the microphone attached to the wooden podium and leaned in. The faint scent of the wood triggered the memory of gripping the cherry wood handle of his favorite Zinger bat as he approached the plate in 2005. He smiled. It was no longer painful to revisit his story. He wasn't angry, ashamed, hurt, or desperate anymore. He was humbled, proud, and motivated. He'd realized how everything that happened to him had been an extraordinary gift. It was a gift he had to share.

Adam's dream of being a Major League Baseball player had been a difficult skin to shed. This epic height had been achieved by less than 20,000 players in all of history. Initially, a career playing the game he loved at that level seemed the height of what existence could offer. When he achieved that dream for only one spectacular and devastating pitch, it obliterated his expectations and altered a trajectory he'd spent his entire life developing. In time, Adam began to see a more profound reality in his life. Once he saw it, an even more epic purpose consumed him. Now he enjoys telling his story because he understands that embedded in all of his suffering is a satisfying and electrifying *why*.

Adam looked out at the rows of young people in front of him eagerly waiting to hear him speak. He began. "I want you guys to go back in your own life and think about the *greatest* thing that has ever happened to you, whatever it is. I want you to really dwell on whatever it was that made you feel that way. I want you to really *feel* that emotion. Remember what it felt like to have such an amazing thing happen to you. Just hold onto that moment okay?"

"Now I'm going to do something I don't normally like to do at all. I want you to think about the *worst* thing that's ever happened to you. I'm not a negative guy so it's hard for me to even say that, but think about something that really hurt, emotionally or physically. I want you to fixate on that emotion, how you felt, what you were going through. Take that most *amazing* feeling and mix it with the terrible feeling, that *terrible* thing that happened. Now imagine what it would feel like if those two things happened, at the *exact same time*. Because that's what happened to me. It's where *our* story begins…"

Adam proceeded to describe his journey. He encouraged all those in attendance to look for opportunity whenever adversity may strike. He challenged them with his keys to perseverance to dismantle all obstacles in pursuit of their dreams. After a wave of applause, a young man near the back of the room quietly stood up and walked toward him. He waited patiently for his turn to speak, and soon all the others moved on.

The high school senior began by thanking Adam. He told him that years earlier he suffered a traumatic brain injury involving a metal rod impaling his head during an accident. Medical personnel encircled him, scrambling to provide treatment while his family grappled with what was happening. His dream was to earn a college basketball scholarship, and he didn't know if it would be possible after his injury. All the fear of those moments were drowned by Adam's One at Bat campaign. The young man described hearing Adam's story on *Today* from his hospital bed as the necessary comfort and motivation he needed to persevere through painful and frustrating physical therapy. He told Adam he just secured a scholarship to play college basketball that fall. Adam realized he had been the young man's teammate in his moment of terrifying trauma, even though he was just now meeting him years later.

Dusty's words echoed in Adam's heart and mind as gratitude flooded within him. *God's got a plan for you, Adam. Don't give up.* If Adam had given up, what may have happened to this talented young athlete standing in front of him? Adam was never a Major League Baseball All-Star. He never hit a home run in a major league game. He never made a diving, game saving catch at Wrigley Field. He never even got to bury his cleats into a major league first base. If, however, the story of Adam's life calmed and soothed a terrified child in an Emergency Room after surviving a traumatic brain injury and inspired him to persevere, then every second of his journey was worth it.

Adam has become able to help others quell their internal storms because of what he survived, much like Dusty Baker did for him. In 2012, a 12-year-old boy named Jared Schwartz stepped into the batter's box during a little league baseball game. The next pitch was inside, and Jared turned toward the umpire in an attempt to avoid it. The ball struck his helmet just behind his right ear. It was identical to how Adam was struck in 2005. Jared's father, frantic at the sight, ran to his son's side. He was shaken to see his son's glassy eyes which resembled a boxer who'd just been knocked out.

Afterward Jared couldn't tolerate the light of television or computer screens. A walk down his driveway exhausted him to the point he needed a four-hour nap to recover. He couldn't play drums anymore because the noise in the band room was overwhelming. Depression set in as he struggled to cope with his symptoms. The horror his parents experienced seeing their son's glassy eyes after being hit by the baseball was eclipsed by the terror of finding him in a closet in his bedroom contemplating suicide. Jared's parents began to search for anyone who could reach their son and help him cope with the trauma of what he was experiencing.

Howard, Jared's father, discovered an article about Adam and found a glimmer of hope. Adam was scheduled to speak at a nearby school so Howard contacted the principal in hopes of getting an autographed picture or something which would help his son to cope with his symptoms. When Adam heard what happened, he got Jared's phone number and called to comfort and assure him that his symptoms would improve. The words resonated with Jared because Adam had experienced the same thing at the highest professional level. Adam encouraged Jared not to give up and to stay positive. He helped him get up.

They remained in touch throughout Jared's rehabilitation process by email, text message, and phone calls. Jared and his family visited Adam while he was playing for the Bridgeport Bluefish, where they shared a game of catch on the field. Adam introduced Jared to Dr. Seiller who helped improve his depth perception. To this day, Jared and his parents are overwhelmed with gratitude for Adam's investment in their child's life. He served as a guiding light that led their family out of a very dark place.

Adam loves building relationships like these. They fuel a humbling satisfaction within him as he forges his own painful experiences into empowerment and inspiration for others. The reward is hearing relief and excitement in young athletes' re-energized voices as they soldier on to overcome trauma and depression. It comes from sharing the fire that carried him from the small town of Guilford, Connecticut, to the worldwide stage of the major leagues with budding entrepreneurs, sports teams, business professionals, and religious organizations. The agonizing pain Adam felt as a result of that fateful pitch was not the destroyer of his life. It was the creative force that gifted him with an ability to empathize and empower others on a global level.

Stephen Hearn is the president and chief executive officer of The Hearn Company, a Chicago-based real estate development firm. Hearn has owned and operated commercial real estate throughout the United States since 1974, developing projects including the John Hancock Center, one of the most iconic skyscrapers in the world. When Adam learned through a friend that Hearn's son was a fan of the Chicago Cubs first baseman Anthony Rizzo,

Adam reached out to those in the organization who could connect them without expecting anything in return. Content to merely share the joy of a young person meeting their professional baseball hero, Hearn sincerely appreciated Adam's selfless act, and they quickly became friends.

"Adam has a moving story without question," he said. "To go through the life-changing experiences he went through and continue to stay focused on the goal he set for himself is inspirational. To come back the way he did – it's powerful. He didn't give up. Lots of people go through setbacks and adversity, and they *never* get up. It becomes a story of 'poor me.'" He believed Adam's story resonates especially with young people growing up today. "Young people are searching for ways to contribute and be relevant. Adam demonstrates to them that if you stay with what you believe in, anything is possible. Regardless of the hand you're dealt, people who persevere, succeed. You have to pay your dues. You don't get to come in right at the top. That's what makes it so enjoyable once you get there. The bitter times make you truly value when things become sweet."

Today, Lurong Living has become the perfect vehicle to channel Adam's all-out style of play on the baseball field into his approach to business. As the CEO, his days and nights are dedicated to investing in the health and success of others as they become physically and mentally fit. It is an honor Adam commits himself to at the highest level. He loves being a positive voice and example of perseverance to those who are giving everything they have to build something significant with their lives. His legacy is investing his life in others who beam with the pride of accomplishing the goals they never thought possible.

In Adam's Own Words…

Everyone experiences adversity, and I'm on a mission to show the world how to embrace the phenomenal opportunities it presents. It whispered to me during desperate moments of pain, disorientation, and confusion. I caught glimpses of it in my family's consistent presence and support. Now, Lindsay and I are the proud parents of a son named Leo and parenting has become our most important role. We enjoy seeing the determined look in Leo's eyes as he figures out the challenges he faces each day. When he falls down, we teach him how to get back up. Although he is only a toddler, we enjoy teaching him values of perseverance, hard work, getting up, getting after his dreams and treating everyone with respect.

Dusty was right. I am instilling the heart and mind of a champion in my son. Leo won't grow up in the dugout of a major league stadium watching me play baseball, but he will grow up watching me travel the world with the goal of empowering and inspiring every single person I meet, which now includes you. Thank you for investing your time and energy in reading about my life. My great hope is that my story will inspire you to persevere to achieve your dreams and goals, no matter what they may be or where you are right now. I look forward to making history together. Nothing will stop us as long as we simply keep getting back up!

– Adam

Adam's Keys to Perseverance

1. Develop a vision so engaging that you're willing to invest your entire life into it.

2. Take action by setting achievable goals to dismantle the obstacles in your way.

3. Proactively seek out and connect with those who can help you achieve your goals.

4. Value integrity and those that have your best interest in mind. Then return the favor.

5. In times of adversity, look for ways to help others get back up. They'll do the same for you.

6. Consciously allow your achievements along the way to fuel faith in the dream before you.

7. Some of the most powerful lessons come from pain. Make it a habit to learn from adversity.

8. When your gut says to keep going, find a way to move forward. Ignore the naysayers.

9. Trust in your dream. Then have patience, it'll be realized when the timing is right.

10. Stay alert for your true calling. It will likely surprise you when and how it arrives.

Selected Sources

"3 Things to Know Before Stealing Second Base." Pro Baseball Insider, probaseballinsider.com/3-things-to-know-before-stealing-second-base/.

"7 Years Later, Marlins Give Adam Greenberg Another Shot." Society for American Baseball Research, sabr.org/latest/7-years-later-marlins-give-adam-greenberg-another-shot.

"A Conversation with Adam Greenberg." GoHeels.com, 26 Apr. 2000, goheels.com/ViewArticle.dbml?ATCLID=205477.

"Adam Greenberg AW-3." Adam Greenberg Baseball Statistics [2000-2013], The Baseball Cube, thebaseballcube.com/players/profile.asp?P=Adam-Greenberg.

"Adam Greenberg Minor, Fall & Independent Leagues Statistics & History." Baseball-Reference.com, baseball-reference.com/register/player.cgi?id=greenb001ada.

"Adam Greenberg Returns to Major Leagues After Hit to Head." ABC News Network, abcnews.go.com/GMA/video/adam-greenberg-returns-major-league-baseball-hit-head-17383079.

"Adam Greenberg Stats, Highlights, Bio | MiLB.Com, milb.com/player/index.jsp?player_id=435279#/career/R/hitting/2012/ALL.

"Adam Greenberg." Jewish Virtual Library, jewishvirtuallibrary.org/adam-greenberg.

"Adam Greenberg: My Seven-Year Quest to Get One More At-Bat in the Major Leagues." SI.com, Sports Illustrated, 2 Oct. 2012, si.com/mlb/2012/10/02/adam-greenberg-marlins.

"BaseballAmerica.com: 2007 Player Statistics: Adam Greenberg." Baseball America, baseballamerica.com/today/stats/player.php?id=435279.

"GUILFORD SPORTS HALL OF FAME: Guilford Welcomes Six Members into Hall of Fame." Shoreline Times, 5 Apr. 2011, shorelinetimes.com/sports/guilford-sports-hall-of-fame-guilford-welcomes-six-members-into/article_0b561c0c-0f50-5840-a839-8caa85d6d40b.html.

"Guillen: Greenberg to play Tuesday for Marlins." ESPN.com, 2 Oct. 2012, espn.go.com/mlb/story/_/id/8450683/ozzie-guillen-says-adam-greenberg-play-tuesday-marlins.

"Jewish Baseball News." Jewish Baseball News Adam Greenberg Tag, Jewish Baseball, 16 Nov. 2016, jewish baseballnews.com/tag/adam-greenberg/.

"Player Bio: Adam Greenberg - University of North Carolina Tar Heels Official Athletic Site." GoHeels.com, goheels.com/ViewArticle.dbml?ATCLID=205673026.

Baxter, Kevin. "Adam Greenberg Took a Hit to the Head but Kept His Heart in Game." Los Angeles Times, 12 Mar. 2013, articles.latimes.com/2013/mar/12/sports/la-sp-adam-greenberg-20130312.

Bearak, Barry. "Head Trip." The New York Times, 24 Mar. 2007, nytimes.com/2007/03/25/magazine/25baseball.t.html.

Bearak, Barry. "Wanted: Jewish Ballplayers." The New York Times, 18 Sept. 2012, nytimes.com/2012/09/19/sports/baseball/team-israel-scouts-for-talent-and-jewish-ties.html.

Berkow, Ira. "Cubs Rookie Recovering from a Debut That Nearly Became an Exit." The New York Times, 22 Aug. 2005, nytimes.com/2005/08/22/sports/baseball/cubs-rookie-recovering-from-a-debut-that-nearly-became-an.html.

Brink, Bill. "Filmmaker Focuses on Greenberg's Shot at 2nd Chance." Pittsburgh Post-Gazette, 14 Sept. 2012, post-gazette.com/pirates/2012/09/14/Filmmaker-focuses-on-Greenberg-s-shot-at-2nd-chance/stories/201209140190.

Brooks, Matt. "Adam Greenberg's 'Magical' Second At-Bat Was Worth the Wait." The Washington Post, 3 Oct. 2012, washingtonpost.com/news/early-lead/wp/2012/10/03/adam-greenbergs-magical-second-at-bat-was-worth-the-wait.

Capozzi, Joe. "Adam Greenberg Signs One-Day Contract with Miami Marlins | Fish Tank blog: Miami Marlins | The Palm Beach Post." 27 Sept. 2012, blogs.palmbeachpost.com/marlins/2012/09/27/adam-greenberg-signs-one-day-contract-with-miami-marlins.

DiComo, Anthony. "Dickey Leaves Door Open in NL Cy Young Race." Major League Baseball, 3 Oct. 2012, m.mlb. com/news/article/39381544.

Everett, Travis. "Baseball Swings by Central Florida." GoHeels.com, Official Site of Carolina Athletics, 28 Jan. 2000, goheels.com/ViewArticle.dbml?ATCLID= 205496229&DB_OEM_ID=3350.

Giannopolous, Angela. "The Most Inspiring Sports Story You'll Read All Year." Men's Health, 22 Nov. 2013, mens health.com/guy-wisdom/the-most-inspiring-sports-story-youll-read-all-year.

Green, Tom. "Adam Greenberg Enjoys 'Magical' Second Chance in Miami." Major League Baseball, 2 Oct. 2012, m.mlb.com/news/article/39363856.

Hanna, Jason. "Batter Beaned in His Only MLB Game Years Ago Gets Another Shot." CNN, 2 Oct. 2012, cnn.com/2012/10/02/sport/baseball-greenberg-second-chance.

Holtzman, Bob. "Greenberg Won't Let Dream Slip Away." ESPN, 16 Mar. 2007, sports.espn.go.com/ mlb/news/story?id=2799439.

Jussim, Matthew. "30 MLB Players Absolutely Crushing Their Offseason Workouts." Men's Fitness, 23 Jan. 2017, mensfitness.com/sports/baseball/30-mlb-players-absolut ely-crushing-their-offseason-workouts.

Kaduk, Kevin. "Adam Greenberg Seeks One Official At-Bat with Help of Campaign and Petition." Yahoo!,

Yahoo!, 30 Aug. 2012, sports.yahoo.com/blogs/mlb-big-league-stew/adam-greenberg-seeks-one-official-bat-help-campaign-171733871--mlb.html.

Kaplan, Ron. "Adam Greenberg: On the Comeback Trail." New Jersey Jewish News, 2 July 2009, njjewishnews.com/njjn.com/070209/sptAdamGreenberg.html.

Keefe, Neil. "Adam Greenberg Opens Up About His 'One At-Bat' with Miami Marlins." CBS Dallas / Fort Worth, 3 Oct. 2012, dfw.cbslocal.com/2012/10/03/adam-greenberg-opens-up-about-his-one-at-bat-with-miami-marlins.

Kepner, Tyler. "Marlins Giving Player His First At-Bat, Seven Years Later." The New York Times, 27 Sept. 2012, nytimes.com/2012/09/28/sports/baseball/marlins-giving-adam-greenberg-his-first-at-bat-seven-years-later.html.

Kyrcz, Sarah Page. "Gala for a Cure Lives on in Melissa Marottoli's Memory to Fight Cancer." New Haven Register, 27 Feb. 2016, nhregister.com/article/NH/20160227/NEWS/160229564.

Liston, Matt. "Adam Greenberg and Matt Liston Enter Marlins Park." YouTube, 2 Oct. 2012, youtube.com/watch?v=PfX3I_YARvE.

Liston, Matt. "MLB Players Offer Their At-Bat." YouTube, 26 Sept. 2012, youtube.com/watch?v=fIWiNipCKGk.

Montgomery, Eric. "Greenberg Singles." Shoreline Times, 28 July 2011, shorelinetimes.com/archive/greenberg-

singles/article_13f130b4-0cee-5a9f-a460-2caf27a9809d.
html.

Posnanski, Joe. "Adam Greenberg Got What All of Us
Want: A Fair Chance." Sports on Earth, 3 Oct. 2012,
sportsonearth.com/article/39419704/adam-greenbergs-
long-at-bat-with-miami-marlins-represents-what-everyone
-wants-fair-chance.

Richardson, Randy. "Second Chances: Adam Greenberg's
Inspirational Baseball Journey." Wrigleyville Nation, 2
Sept. 2014, wrigleyvillenation.com/2014/09/02/
second-chances-adam-greenbergs-inspirational-
baseball-journey.

Rome, Jim (@jimrome). "Adam Greenberg gets his first
at-bat in SEVEN YEARS, and has to face a KNUCKLE
BALLER? Who won 20 games?! What kind of a sick joke is
that?!" 2 Oct. 2012, 10:28 PM. Tweet.

Seiller, Barry. "Sports Vision Performance Training - The
Science of VEPT." Vizual Edge, vizualedge.com/vision-
performance-training/science-of-sports-vision.

Stock, Christopher. "Seven Years Later, Greenberg Strikes
out in First Major League At-Bat." Chicago Tribune /
Sports Exchange, 2 Oct. 2012, chicagotribune.com/
sports/breaking/chi-seven-years-later-greenberg-
strikes-out-in-first-major-league-atbat-20121002,0,992614.
story.

Stump, Scott. "Injured Baseball Player Gets a Second
Chance." *Today* News, NBC, 27 Sept. 2012, today.com/id/
49192759/ns/today-today_news/t/injured-baseball-playe

r-gets-second-chance.

Weinbaum, William. "Adam Greenberg to Get 2nd Chance." ESPN, 27 Sept. 2012, espn.com/mlb/story/_/id/8430448/7-years-later-miami-marlins-give-adam-greenberg-another-bat.

Weiner, Jonah. "Jerry Seinfeld Intends to Die Standing Up." New York Times Magazine, 20 Dec. 2012, nytimes.com/2012/12/23/magazine/jerry-seinfeld-intends-to-die-standing-up.html.

Wineburg, Raffi. "Adam Greenberg Inducted into National Jewish Sports Hall of Fame." Jewish Telegraphic Agency, 16 Sept. 2014, jta.org/2014/09/16/news-opinion/the-telegraph/adam-greenberg-inducted-into-national-jewish-sports-hall-of-fame.

About the Authors

Adam Greenberg: If there's ever a person who epitomizes perseverance, it's Adam Greenberg, famous for the one pitch that changed his life forever. A 92 mile-an-hour first-pitch fastball to the back of the head on his major league debut with the Chicago Cubs gave Adam the record for being one of only two players in history to have an official at-bat without ever taking the field. After seven years of continued hustle to get back, Adam signed a one-day contract with the Miami Marlins in 2012. He was inducted into the National Jewish Sports Hall of Fame in 2014. Adam is an All-State native of Connecticut and an All-American standout at the University of North Carolina at Chapel Hill. In 2010, he founded the health and wellness company Lurong Living, where he enjoys empowering others to gain control of their health through a line of dietary supplements and nationwide health challenges. As a proven dynamic leader, he also enjoys traveling the country sharing his story and keys to perseverance.

Ben Biddick: After attending the University of Wisconsin, Ben Biddick enlisted in the United States Army following the terror attacks of September 11, 2001. He served as a combat medic and military policeman in Iraq and performed Emergency Management operations for the State of Wisconsin. Following military service, Biddick served as a civilian law enforcement officer focused upon the prevention of domestic violence, the exploitation of children in the form of human trafficking, and criminal gang membership. He also served as a Crisis and Hostage Negotiator. He is an author, public speaker, and consultant who strives to transform the effects of trauma into power bases of positive change, recovery, and empowerment. As the owner of Ideal State Consulting LLC, he uses his Master's Degree in Performance Improvement and experiences to assist individuals and organizations to create a more just and noble America worthy of the honorable men and women who built it and continue to build it every day.

Made in the USA
San Bernardino, CA
24 August 2017